Water Bath Canning & Preserving (Beginners

Uncover the Ancestors' Secrets to Become Self-Sufficient in an Affordable Way and Create your 1000 Days Survival Food Storage

Copyright © 2022

Sarah Roslin

TABLE OF CONTENTS

1 THE BASICS OF BARIATRIC SURGERY

Are you excited about prepping for an emergency but struggling to learn how to do it?

Are you worried about your family's food supplies, fishing catches, and neighbors not coming through when you need them?

If you answered yes to any of these questions, this book is for you! This book will teach you everything important in learning how to preserve food.

If you've ever wondered what pressure canning, water bath canning, and fermenting are all about, you've come to the right place. We'll review the differences between these techniques and why they benefit the prepper's survival plan.

This book will teach you how to preserve food regardless of your skill level. You will get the ins and outs of preserving food. Novices make plenty of mistakes when preserving food; if you do the same thing, it could end up being ruined.

You will learn the tools and equipment you will need to complete this job and the mistakes beginners make while preserving food.

If you are an experienced prepper reading this, you too can benefit from this book. If you have ever eaten grass-fed beef and nuts or made your sauerkraut, then you know what it is like knowing how to preserve food. This book compiles everything I learned through trial and error. Now you don't have to do that.

This book is not just a beginner's guide. Instead, this book will teach you how to preserve food regardless of age, skills or experience.

If you are a prepper then this book is for you. Of course, you already know how important it is to have food for your family and friends when SHTF, but did you know that preserving food helps you reach your goal faster?

Preserving food also reduces waste. If you have ever bought a 30-pound bag of rice, you know how much space that can take up. Preserving food helps reduce the amount of food waste by as much as 60%!

The information in this book is worth more. It will save you time and money in the end. I am sure that you will at least break even if not make a profit when you are done preserving all of your food!

All of the information in this book is based on first-hand experience. Unfortunately, I was one of those who had to learn how to preserve food the hard way.

After a while, I realized there were many others out there like me and started to write an eBook about my experiences. Over time, it grew into what you see today.

Although home canning and preserving is difficult, you can still prepare plenty of food and store it for years. For example, you can make jams and jellies from fruits. These jams are sweet and are high in sugar. However, these jams and jellies are excellent ways to add fruit to your diet. Some items you cannot safely include in your emergency food stash are noodles and other ingredients for soups.

This book will teach you everything you need to know to preserve food. So what are you waiting for? Press the BUY NOW button and let's begin!

2 AN OVERVIEW INTO CANNING TECHNIQUES

Have you ever wondered what is the process of canning food? There are several benefits to canning your food, and there are several types of jars to choose from.

Canning and preserving foods is an important skill for any homesteader or prepper. You can save money by preserving foods, and water bath canning is the easiest method. In addition, there are no specialized gear required to perform this task. All you need is a large pot, rack, canning jars, lids, and acidic foods. Learn more about water bath canning.

Home canning goes back to the Napoleonic Wars, when Napoleon needed to feed his army on a budget. The process has changed and become safer, but the basic principles of home canning remain the same. The process of canning is the same today as it was when Nicholas Appert invented the process in 1809. The main ingredient in canned foods is heat, which kills microorganisms. Heat is used to sterilize foods at a temperature of 240 to 250 degrees Fahrenheit (116 to 121 degrees Celsius). The process time varies according to the food's acidity, density and ability to transfer heat. Foods like corn and pumpkin require longer processing than tomatoes.

Modern canning is a highly efficient method of preserving food. It involves sanitizing containers and sealing food within them. The optimal temperature destroys spoilage organisms and pathogenic bacteria without compromising the nutritional and physical quality of the food. The principles of canning apply to different containers, which can be rectangular, oval, or cylindrical. And because it is a time-consuming process, many people opt for it over commercially-produced products.

The primary goal of canning is to preserve food by killing the microorganisms and keeping the food safe from future spoilage. It involves placing food into jars, sealing them, and then applying high heat to the jars. This heat kills the microorganisms and inactivates the enzymes causing food to spoil. After the process is complete, the food has a shelf life that lasts for years. The only problem is that you need a canning method to keep your food at a certain temperature long enough to kill all microorganisms.

Another goal of canning is to seal the food air tight so that no air or microorganisms can enter or escape. This will prevent your food from spoiling.

The process of canning dates back to the late eighteenth century. The process was developed by Nicholas Appert, who discovered that sealing food with heat prevented its spoilage. Peter Durand and Bryan Dorkin, who settled in New York, improved the same concept. The process gained widespread acceptance when Louis Pasteur demonstrated that the growth of microorganisms causes food spoilage.

The canning process includes several stages. First, raw foods are cleaned, blanched, filled under vacuum, sterilized, and labeled. Depending on the product, the process could last anywhere from one day to several months. Traditionally, meats and fish were cooked until their flesh softened. They are then separated from bones and placed in cans with appropriate liquid. The process can also be automated. In modern canneries, the raw food is filtered and washed.

If you plan to start home canning and preserving food, you need to invest in good canning jars. You can purchase jars of different sizes and shapes, but remember that quart and pint size are the most appropriate for most types of food. When it comes to the size of your jars, you should avoid making jam in anything larger than a pint or quart.

In a nutshell, canning is the process of transforming the ingredients into a stable, long-lasting form. The whole process is highly satisfying, and far more enjoyable than the average grocery store visit. Additionally, canning gives you more control over what goes into your canned food, because you can often use better quality, home-grown ingredients.

Whether you are beginning to prepper or have been doing it for years, this chapter will teach you the basics and most useful information you need to know so that your canned food doesn't end up in the trash.

2.1 Benefits of Canning Your Food

Canning your food is a great way to preserve nutrients and reduce energy costs. The process of canning can also preserve foods with the highest nutritional value. Canned foods are as nutritious as fresh and frozen foods, but the process preserves more of these nutrients and protects them from bacteria. Canned foods also contain the same levels of minerals, vitamins, protein, and carbohydrates as fresh foods.

Home canning and preserving are an excellent way to stock your food supply in an emergency for self-reliant folks. Home canning is both rewarding and safe. You can use the food you make to supplement your diet and are also a good steward of the environment and your local economy. Home canned foods will also save you money over time, because they are stored in reusable jars. Grocery stores are often packed with wasteful packaging, making it impossible to use them again.

You can add whatever you like to your home-canned food, which is a huge plus. You can use organic produce and reduce sugar content for a healthier snack. Also, you can add herbs and spices to vegetables and fruits, like a homemade jam with habanero chili. As a result, you can create a unique flavor profile for your food. The process of canning is a rewarding experience.

Another benefit of canning is the environmental benefit. You are reducing the amount of waste created by pre-packaged foods. For example, a single can of tomato sauce must only travel a few miles to reach your pantry, instead of thousands of miles in a truck. Also, cans of food are much cheaper to make than commercially prepared foods, because produce is available in season and inexpensive. You can even recreate jams and preserves at home for pennies on the dollar!

One of the primary reasons to preserve foods at home is to reduce energy and food costs. Food production and transportation use a lot of energy. In addition, the highly industrialized food industry relies heavily on pesticides, herbicides, and petrochemical fertilizers. These chemicals degrade soil, causing increased food scarcity and increased commodity prices. Home canning and preserving also helps reduce exposure to harmful chemicals, such as Bisphenol A.

Canned fruit and vegetables are healthier than canned juice and rich in antioxidants and other nutrients. When canned, the nutrients are preserved longer and taste better than the fresh ones. Also, you can use various cans for a wide range of foods. For instance, you can prepare homemade jam using 7 cups sugar and 5 cups strawberries. However, this jam tastes more like candy and contains too much sugar. Sugar contributes to obesity and other health problems, which is why most first world countries suffer from an obesity epidemic. In addition, too much sodium has been associated with many ailments, including heart disease, high blood pressure, and kidney disease.

Another reason to have canned foods stored at home is convenience. Home canned foods are convenient for a variety of reasons. First, you can store them in your pantry or freezer, which can be purchased wherever you buy food. They are made of heavy aluminum with a wax interior. It is possible to buy these food products in bulk, so you can rotate your supplies at home. And because they are so convenient, many people are opting for them.

Besides its low cost and convenience, canned foods have an extended shelf life. These cans can last from one to five years, which is a considerable benefit if you have a tendency to throw away fresh produce. Additionally, canned food can be frozen, so you'll never have to worry about the food spoilage. These are just a few of the benefits of canning your food.

2.2 Types of Canning

There are several types of canning. One is traditional canning, where a product is canned in glass jars. The retort is another type of canning equipment. In addition to the retort, this equipment requires a steam supply system, a condensate removal system, and product containers. In addition, a steam-and-air circulation system and valves, spreaders, and mufflers are required. A retort must also have a heating system for the steam and air and a condensate removal system. Then, the product is packaged and placed into the retort.

When selecting what types of food to can, consider the season. For example, if your favorite food is a summer fruit, you may want to consider making plum jam. Plums are plentiful and relatively inexpensive in the summer, so you may wish to invest in this canning method. You can also create hot pepper jam in the fall, citrus curd, or marmalade during winter. And in spring, you might want to try pickling asparagus.

Water bath canning is another option. This method requires less acidic foods such as tomatoes. On the other hand, pressure canning is suitable for all types of food, including non-acidic foods. The main difference between water bath and pressure canning is the type of acidity. Pressure canning uses more pressure than a water bath canner, and can be used for fruit, vegetables, and other foods.

Conventional canning requires high temperatures and a longer shelf life. However, this method is energy-intensive, and the food degrades in quality and nutritional content over time. In addition, conventional canning requires a lot of heat and time for sterilization. Therefore, this method isn't recommended for sensitive individuals with allergies or those on a special diet. Nonetheless, it is the most convenient method for many people.

The traditional canner is a metal container that has the name "can." It has no risks of breaking and is the most common method for canning. It is the most common canning method suitable for wet and dry-packed foods. And it's the most popular and efficient one. But, you can also use glass jars for canning. There are many other types of canners, so it's important to research which method is best for your cooking needs.

Why Preserve Food?

It can be tempting to skip the preservative step when shopping for fresh produce. While you don't have to throw out perfectly good food immediately, there are plenty of ways to preserve your food for later. These methods include fermentation, freezing, and salting. Read on to learn more. After all, these techniques save money, and you'll be happy you did. If you're unsure where to start, check out our handy guides.

Canning

You can make delicious foods for your family by canning. Canning is the process of preserving food in jars. It is much easier than you might think.

Freezing

One of the oldest methods of preserving food is freezing. It has many benefits, including the preservation of texture, taste, and nutritional value. In addition, its combination of low temperatures, slow chemical reactions, and postponement of cellular metabolic changes prevents the growth of harmful microorganisms. Nevertheless, freezing is not always the most effective way to preserve food. Nevertheless, its benefits are still worth considering. Here's how freezing works.

Fermenting

Fermenting food is a natural process that has been used for thousands of years. Many foods and beverages can be preserved this way. However, this process can produce harmful organisms. Failure to sterilize vessels and equipment can increase the risk of food-borne illness. Discoloration and off-flavors are signs that harmful bacteria are present in the food. To avoid this situation, you should always use sterile equipment before beginning the fermentation process.

Salting

Throughout history, humans have used various methods to preserve food. Salt, sugar and vinegar have been used as preservation methods for thousands of years. Bacon was preserved with salt in Ancient Rome. The Egyptians used earthenware jars for salting. The Gauls used wooden kegs. And, during the Middle Ages, wooden salting chests were a common feature of kitchens. Salt was an important part of preservation methods in pre-industrial times, with two-thirds of the salt being used for this purpose.

Dehydrating

Although dehydrating decreases the water content of food, the dehydrated food has similar nutritional value to the original. However, the process can cause some food items more likely to cause overeating, so dehydrated foods should be consumed in moderation. There are several benefits to dehydrating food. Listed below are some of the benefits of dehydrating your food. A jar of dehydrated food will be about half the size of a fresh one.

2.3 What is water bath canning?

Water bath canning is one of the most common methods of preserving foods. It is an excellent way to extend the shelf life of foods such as pickles, jams, preserves, and pie fillings. This method also makes food storage much easier, reducing the amount of trash produced from plastic water bottles. However, water in jars ages quickly. After a few months, it develops an off taste and starts to attract moss and mold.

Preparation is essential for successful water bath canning. First, you need to pre-heat the pot. You can use any type of rack. Make sure the pot is at about 200 degrees Fahrenheit. Once the water is at the correct temperature, place the jars in the pot. Once they are hot, remove the jars from the water bath. Once the jars have cooled down, put them in the refrigerator.

When canning, you should boil your potable water to 180 degrees F. You should fill clean jars with the boiling water, leaving 1/2 inch headspace. Seal them tightly using finger-tight canning lids. Next, place the jars in the water bath canner. If you have a large pot, ensure the jar is in the correct place.

Canning is one of the most useful skills to have as a prepper. It can save you a lot of money compared to buying preparedness food. Fortunately, the water bath method is easy to learn and requires no special equipment. All you need is a large pot to hold your canned items, a rack, and some jars with lids. You can buy everything you need for water bath canning at home or on the internet.

Water bath canning is the easiest way to preserve food. Most canned goods can be prepared with a water bath. Some foods, such as fruits, must be canned in a pressure canner. This canner features a lid that seals in steam during the process, which is nice to have in hot weather. Large enough jars for a family can be processed in water bath canning.

A water bath canner is an essential tool for preserving your food, but if you're new to this process, here are some water bath canning basics. This large pot can be used for small batches. It should fit inside a larger stockpot. You'll need a canning rack to fit inside the stockpot. The process depends on the food you're canning, so read the recipe carefully.

Before you begin, ensure your canning area is clean and tidy. Wipe down counters. Use clean, soft cloths and towels when preparing food. Prepare fruits and vegetables. Preparations may include washing, peeling, dicing, or crushing. If you're using canned products, label them with the batch number. Once the jars are completed, store them in a cool, dry place. You can use them within a year.

While boiling-water canning is easier, it's not for every food. This process is best suited for foods with high acid levels, like tomatoes. The high acid content helps prevent bad bacteria from growing. However, newer tomato hybrids don't have enough acid content to water-bath canning. Fortunately, water-bath canners aren't that difficult to use.

The water level in a pressure canner must be at least one inch above the jars. The jars can then be removed from the pressure canner once cooled. A thick towel or wooden cutting board can be used to cool them. This method can be used for preparing foods for a cold or a hurricane situation. However, if you plan to cook large quantities of food, you'll need a pressure canner.

After washing the jars in hot soapy water, rinse them thoroughly, and place them inside the canner. Cover the canner with hot tap water, and bring it to a simmer. The water should simmer for at least 10 minutes, but not longer. When it's done simmering, the jars should be removed and placed on a heat-proof surface. You can then proceed to filling the jars. You should remember to leave a half-inch headspace between the jars and the lid, as this will prevent slid jars.

2.3.1 Step by step

If you're planning on bottling or preserving foods, you need to be aware of some key things that you need to consider. First of all, canning recipes must maintain a specific pH level. Any deviation from that level can lead to foods being unsafe to eat or becoming too acidic. Water bath techniques are a great option to preserve the bounty of summer. Read on to learn more.

Once you have decided to try water bath canning, you'll need to prepare your produce and supplies. First, wash the jars and lids in hot water with soap. Also, ensure they're completely clean, as they will be exposed to the heat of the water bath. Finally, purchase new lids for every jar, as used lids will leak.

When it comes to acidic foods, you'll want to use a water bath canning method. This method will preserve them at a high enough temperature to kill off microorganisms. It's a good choice for tomatoes and other high-acid foods. Using a water bath will also help seal the jar, preventing bacteria from growing on the food. When done correctly, this method preserves the food for up to 18 months.

The basic technique of boiling water bath canning is the easiest way to store jars. You can preserve savory and sweet foods like jams and pickles. However, water bath canning is the best choice for high-acid foods, such as most preserves and fruit canned in syrup. A trusted recipe is the key to success. Make sure to use sterilized jars and lids for water bath canning.

Before you begin, purchase jars that are the correct size and shape. You can find novelty jars at specialty stores, but remember that they may not be compatible with the exact process times and temperatures. Also, remember that the recommended lid comprises a sealing compound to the outer edge, a metal disk, and a separate metal screw band. These jars can be used repeatedly, as long as the band is not damaged or rusted.

Before beginning water bath canning, you should have a good stockpot. The water in the stockpot should be at least half full. The temperature should remain around a simmer. This will eliminate bacteria. Also, jar lids should be placed on the jars in the water bath for 10 minutes. Jar rings do not need to be boiled. Using the proper water bath canner for preserving food will guarantee that your jars have a long shelf-life.

While tomatoes have naturally high acidity, they are now on the border between low and high acid. Therefore, you must use citric acid, bottled lemon juice, or vinegar to increase their acidity level to at least 5 percent. High-acid foods are fermented vegetables, pickled vegetables, and jams. You can take classes or purchase books if you have a canning kit.

2.4 What is pressure canning?

Pressure canning is a method for preserving food. Pressure canners can process a variety of foods. Depending on the type of food, different canning times are needed. If you are using a large jar, it is best to follow the processing time for the largest ingredient. This way, you will ensure the seal is complete. If you are using a smaller jar, you may want to process it for less time.

When preparing to pressure can your foods, you should ensure that you have the proper equipment. A pressure canner has a dial gauge to monitor the process. You can find the instructions for your particular pressure canner online or contact the manufacturer. The dial gauge should be checked annually. To find a test location near you, visit your state Cooperative Extension office or go online. You can also contact the manufacturers of pressure canners and jars and have it tested by an experienced canner technician.

Before starting pressure canning, you need to set the appropriate time. Most recipes call for setting the pressure to 10 pounds. You need to watch the pressure closely and restart the timer if necessary. The canner is ready to use when you have achieved the desired pressure. A pressure canner should be used for preserving food that has not been tainted by excessive acidity. The USDA recommends you use a pressure canner that contains a pressure gauge.

If you want to preserve foods by pressure canning, you will need a reference book or online tutorial to learn the process. However, there are many benefits to this method of preserving food. Pressure canning allows you to preserve foods with lower pH levels and prevent botulism. Besides saving money, pressure canning reduces the environmental impact of food production. There are also plenty of recipes for pressure canning.

A pressure canner looks like a regular can and is equipped with a locking lid. The lid is equipped with a dial or weighted gauge to accurately control the pressure level in the can. Once the lid is closed, steam is pumped into the container to scan the food and kill microorganisms. Water bath canners are limited to 212 degrees, which is too low a temperature to kill botulism spores.

2.5 What is fermenting?

Fermentation is a process in which organic substances undergo chemical changes through the activity of enzymes. In simpler terms, fermentation involves energy extraction from carbohydrates without oxygen. It occurs in many biological processes, including animal feeding, cheese-making, and wine-making. However, many people do not fully understand what fermentation is. If you have any doubts, read on to find out what it is and why it is so important to our food production.

Fermentation is an ancient process in which bacteria break down organic substrates into usable energy and other compounds. It improves the enzyme content in food, making it easier to digest and absorb nutrients. It also increases the amount of vitamins, minerals, and usable protein. In addition, it enhances the flavor and aroma of foods and improves their shelf life. Fermented foods are widely used today to make everything from cheese to bread and beverages.

To begin the process, peel and chop your vegetables. Ideally, the pieces should be uniform in size to ferment at the same rate. Also, you should carefully weight your vegetables, so their weight is proportional to their volume. For dense vegetables, you should cut them into small slices or dice them. Finally, remember to place them in a fully submerged container in the brine. If you leave them above the brine, they will spoil.

Fermenting is a natural process similar to winemaking but does not require specialized equipment. During lacto-fermentation, bacteria feed on carbohydrates and sugars and produce lactic acid. Fermented produce needs water, a starter culture, and an anaerobic environment. Then, you can start the fermentation process.

Many fermented foods begin by being packed in salt. In the case of sauerkraut, the cabbage is packed with salt and allowed to ferment. Another popular fermented food is kimchi, which is a Korean fermented cabbage. Both have high salt and flavor ingredients and are made with the same technique. However, the process differs in terms of the end product. Regardless of the food you choose to ferment, you should find recipes for many of these products.

2.6 What is sterilization?

In the laboratory, a wide variety of microbes live. Hence, sterilization is necessary to control their environment. Sterilization is a process to destroy those microbes. There are many methods of sterilization, each with its benefits and drawbacks. For example, steam sterilization does not kill bacteria, but it does kill spores. So, what is sterilization and why is it needed?

The word sterilization means to make something completely clean, using a method that will kill germs and microorganisms.

Sterilization techniques vary from the traditional steam under pressure method to a combination of liquid chemical agents. Sometimes, heat is used with ethylene oxide gas or plasma sterilization. In other instances, chemical agents like ethanol and peracetic acid are used to render items sterile. These agents are known to kill microbial cells and spores.

Sterilizing is done through heat, which will kill any microorganisms or bacteria within your food. The only problem is that you must maintain the temperature long enough to kill all microorganisms. This means that it is not enough to just boil food. Instead, you can cook food, but you still have to kill the microorganisms through heat or other methods.

According to the National Center for Home Food Preservation, sterilization is the process of making food safe to be preserved by killing microorganisms that cause spoilage.

With home canning, you sterilize your jars and lids to prevent spoilage. However, jars and lids can't be reused after they have been sterilized, so you must do this step correctly.

Before processing preserves in a boiling-water canner, you must sterilize jars. To sterilize glass jars, place them in boiling water for 10 minutes. Then remove them carefully with jar lifters or tongs. The jars can pick up bacteria and other particles from the surface they're placed on, so make sure you use a clean dish towel to wipe them down.

First, you need to purchase jars. A large stockpot is recommended if you plan on canning more than five jars at a time. Otherwise, you can use your existing canning equipment. You can use a stockpot for small batches. A measuring stick is useful for measuring headspace and air bubbles. Use a stockpot as a canner if you don't have a crock pot.

Using a hot water bath for canning can result in high-quality canned goods. However, it can be dangerous to foods that have not been properly sterilized. It's also possible to create bacteria if the food isn't properly sterilized. Water bath canning should be performed on an electric or gas stovetop. Water bath canning can't be done in the dishwasher or microwave. The jars and lids must be sterilized before the food is processed. Boiling water isn't enough to sterilize food. The boiling water also will not prevent the growth of bacteria in the jars.

Using a canner is not an easy task. A canner should be kept at a temperature of 180 degrees F for maximum sterilization. The water in the canner should also be 180 degrees F. The water should be sterile to reduce the risk of breakage during filling. When the food is ready to be stored, it is best to remove the lid.

2.7 What is preserving?

Water bath canning is a good way to start if you want to learn more about preserving foods in jars. With water bath canning, high acid foods are preserved in jars. Acidic foods are packed into jars with a lid loosely sealed and heated until they are set to the right temperature. The foods that can be canned using this method include jams, apple sauce, tomato products with additional acid, pickles, and relishes. In addition, home canning is a great way to store seasonal produce and preserve them in jars. Here are seven steps to water bath canning:

When you're ready to can your food, you need to choose the right type of canning method. Classic water bath canning is the easiest method and is ideal for most types of preserved foods. It ensures that your food is properly sterilized while you're preserving it. For example, water bath canning is an excellent choice for jams and jellies, since they don't require a hot water bath. But for pickles and relishes, a water bath is important.

The most popular water bath canning method is used for tomatoes, pickles, and fruits. You need to remember that the water in the jam jars will serve as a barrier for the food you're preserving. However, be careful about how much acid you add to the water before sealing the jars. A high acid environment is unfriendly to bacteria, mould, and yeast.

While water bath canning is a popular method of home preserving, it can be difficult for beginners. Inexperienced canners should start with canned goods. You may make some jams and jellies yourself. You can even make jars of jams and jellies and store them in your refrigerator or freezer for years. Water bath canning is a great option if you are serious about preserving food.

2.8 How to Choose the Right Canning Jar

If you are new to home canning, choosing the right canning jars can be a daunting task. Selecting the wrong size can ruin your canned goods and could be dangerous if it breaks. Here are some tips for choosing the right canning jar size.

16

Make sure to check the size of your jars before you buy them. In addition, you can use a mason jar size chart to determine which type of jar is best for your needs.

While several types of jars are available, you will probably need a quart size to process most foods. However, a half pint jar is a great choice for jams and jellies. You can even find decorative jars for your favorite recipes! When you purchase a canning jar, make sure it's the correct size for the food you're preserving.

Glass canning jars are durable and recyclable. They feature markings to ensure that you measure the correct volume for your recipe accurately. Plus, glass jars look great as decor or gift-giving. They take up little space and are reusable endlessly. Wide mouth designs make filling easy and prevent spills. They can also be used to store leftover food or as storage jars! And don't forget that the right canning jar can improve your cooking experience!

Once you have chosen the type of jar that suits your needs, make sure you have a reusable lid for the jar. Most canning jar lids are designed for single use and won't provide a proper seal if you reuse them. The same goes for the jar rings. Choose ones that can be reused numerous times without showing signs of rust. There are many brands and styles of jars on the market.

The jar size you use will depend on the food you plan to preserve. Different jar sizes have different processing times. For example, you may need a smaller jar for a fruit preserve, while a quart jar is ideal for making jams and jellies. Half gallon jars are only suitable for foods with a high acid content. It's best to stick to the recommended jar size for your recipe, which you can find in your recipe book.

3 FOOD KNOWLEDGE BEFORE STARTING

What is the Shelf Life of Canned Food?

Cans and jars of canned food have a very long shelf life, so how do you tell if your canned goods are still good? Most cans come with a "use-by" date stamped on the label. These are the dates that the manufacturers have chosen, but there is often a difference between what the date says and what it means. For example, canned fruits and vegetables may remain fresh for up to two years, but if they are over two years old, they might no longer be edible. Cans are not only safe to eat, but they also help preserve food flavors. They can last for years when properly stored and refrigerated. Typically, canned goods have a shelf life of three to five years. But, packaged foods, such as soups, sauces, and fruits, will lose quality after the 'best-by' date, so it's important to use up canned goods before their 'use-by' date. A good rule of thumb is to use older cans first. Then, after opening them, check them to ensure they are intact and free of any damage. Discard cans that spurt or have an odor or look that don't make sense should be thrown away. Ideally, you should use older cans and keep the newest ones in the front of the pantry. This way, you can easily find the best-quality cans for your family. The shelf life of canned foods is determined by the conditions under which they are stored. In the right conditions, canned foods can last up to a century, which is far longer than the timeframe that most people believe. For example, the famous steamboat Bertrand sank on the Missouri River in 1865, but luckily, its canned food was recovered in 1968. Researchers analyzed the recovered food for contaminants and nutrient value. The shelf life of canned goods depends on whether they are high-acid or low-acid. Low-acid canned foods can be kept for 1.5 years, while high-acid cans can keep for 5 years. While cans do not grow bacteria, they will lose texture and may need refreshing periodically. While there is no way to tell how long your canned food will remain good, it's still best to refrigerate and eat them before expiration.

3.1 Understanding the Temperature and Time

To understand the temperature and time of canning, we need to know how food is processed. The temperature is raised to the lethal level during the processing phase, and then is maintained at that level for the required time to kill any spoilage organism. The temperature-time relationship is crucial to the process, as it allows the manufacturer to calculate the total time necessary to destroy all known spoilage organisms. The temperature-time relationship can be calculated by plotting temperature against time on coordinate paper. The initial temperature is the temperature reached during the process, as the steam-pressure canner reaches the required 240 deg F. It is distinguished from the packing and sealing temperatures. The temperature and time required to sterilize canning food are described in a series of guidelines published by William Underwood and Samuel C. Prescott. The temperature requirements are critical because they prevent food from becoming contaminated and maintain the integrity of the canning vessel. This information can be found in the processing section of a canning recipe. You should not follow a canning recipe that does not specify the correct temperature and time for sterilization. The temperatures and times used in canning can vary from manufacturer to manufacturer. Generally, the heating treatment should be at 121 degC or more for two minutes. This will kill the mesophilic microorganisms in the food. For example, a 12-log10 reduction in Clostridium botulinum spores will be achieved in two minutes. While the process time and temperature may seem insignificant, they can impact the quality of food products. The importance of maintaining a constant temperature during the canning process cannot be overemphasized. Early research involved measuring the maximum temperature reached with a thermocouple hidden in the can and maintaining that temperature long enough to kill off all spoilage organisms. But today, we can use a thermocouple to measure the temperature changes inside the jars using an accurate and reliable method.

3.2 Understanding Acidity

The first step to safely can fruit is to understand the PH level. Fruit should have a pH level of 4.6 or less. A lower number indicates more acidity. An acidic environment prevents botulism spores from germination. Therefore, a water bath canner must maintain an acid level of 4.6 or lower to prevent botulism growth. When using an acidic water bath canner, the acid will dissolve any pectin in the fruit. There are several methods to determine the pH of a food. Some experts use a PRAL scale, while others make approximations based on the pH of various foods. For example, lemon is considered high acid when canned, even though it contains hydrogen-rich citric acid. However, this hardly means lemons are acidic. Consider the following examples to understand the pH values in a specific food. High acid foods contain a high concentration of hydrogen ions. These include fruits, juices, pickled foods, and fermented foods. For example, adding bacon to strawberry jam will change the food's pH value from high to low. Because of this, knowing the exact pH of a particular mixture is impossible without knowing a little about acid-base chemistry. In addition, it is important to remember your ingredients' pH value when making homemade jam. In addition to proper temperature and acidity, it is important to consider the presence of mold or yeast. Mold and yeast, which require oxygen to grow, will destroy the food in high-acid conditions. They can also cause the food to swell. In this case, it is advisable to discard the canning container if you notice any signs of mold or yeast. A healthy pH level will help prevent botulism. While it is impossible to fully control the pH level in a recipe, you can use acidifiers like vinegar, lemon juice, or lime juice to raise it. These ingredients will reduce the acidity of your canned goods and may even add flavor if given some time to rest in the fridge. This is especially important for wine, which has a natural pH level of 3.0 to 4.0 and should not be canned in a water bath.

Relation between PH of foods and the temperature that is used to destroy bacteria

In water bath canning, the heat is applied directly only to the food, just like for freezing. So the PH (potential of hydrogen) in foods being processed does not change, whatever it is you are contrasting against.

The temperatures used in water bath canning, which vary from 10-120°F (50 – 50°C) produce hot water, which may or may not be boiling on the jar's surface, depending on your process and jar size. It's the hot water bath that does the work of killing the bacteria, not the PH of the food. Any bacteria on or in your food will die if you get to those critical temperatures. And by "critical" temperatures, I mean the temperature at which your canning jar contents become "sterilized" and no more active microorganisms will survive in there. So it's a sterile environment inside that canning jar when it comes out of that hot water bath. PH of foods is not important, in water bath canning. Instead, how you treat your food before putting it in jars is what matters. The higher the pH (lower PH value), the more acid there is in your food, and the more antimicrobial properties (and wait for it…) your food will have. That's right – the less alkaline your food is when you start canning, the better off you are! This applies to water bath canning. So, the more acidic your food is when you start heating it in water bath canning, the better off you are. So, if it's low acid food that you are starting with (like tomato sauce), you've got a nice head start. Other factors to consider:

1. The microbial load of the food
2. The conditions of your environment
3. The amount of time that the food will be pasteurized in the water bath canner

3.3 Importance of Altitude

The altitude at which you live will affect the canning process. Water boiling points are lower at altitudes above 1,000 feet, so you must adjust your recipe accordingly. If you live in a high-altitude region, you should consult a canning altitude chart to get the right processing time. If you are unsure how to adjust a recipe for altitude, start with a simple recipe. Your altitude will affect how long your water bath must process the food. Recipes state the number of minutes your jars must be processed at a specific temperature to kill the bacteria that cause spoilage. However, the actual processing time will depend on your altitude, and you should increase the time accordingly. Here are some tips to ensure the success of your process: high-altitude conditions should be considered when selecting your food preparation methods. You should always check the instructions for processing times for your altitude to ensure that your food is properly preserved and safe for your family. You will also need to adjust your cooking time as well. If you live at a higher altitude, you should adjust your processing time by 5 minutes. If you live in a high-altitude region, you should avoid pressure canning, which uses pounds of pressure.

4 HOW TO WATER BATH CAN IN 4 EASY STEPS

4.1 Step 1: Preparation

First, you should ensure that the jars are clean, rinsed and ready to be filled with food. The next step is to ensure that your canning lids and rings are clean. This will allow you to properly seal them so that air can't escape or enter.

You should also boil your lids before you begin heating them in water. Jars without lids or rings will not produce a vacuum seal, which means you will end up with a leaky jar of spoiled food.

You will also want to fill your canning pot with water, as this is where you will keep the jars for the entirety of the project. All the jars must be covered with water, so you must have a large enough pot and enough water to cover all of your jars.

You must sterilize all kitchen equipment before you begin canning food, including: pot, spoons, tongs and any other equipment you use.

4.2 Step 2: Heating

After filling the jars and checking them for air bubbles, you will heat them to a high enough temperature to kill all the microorganisms.

The next step is putting all the jars in the canning pot and then filling it with water. The water level needs to be high enough to cover all of the jars, so you may need extra water depending on how many jars you are preserving food with.

Once your jars are in the boiling water, start timing your process. The more water you have, the longer your process will take. The ideal time for canning is as long as necessary to ensure that your food is sterilized and is safe for consumption.

You will need to start timing your process immediately after heating the jars in boiling water. You do not have to wait until the water reaches a boiling point, but you will want to ensure it doesn't get above 212 degrees Fahrenheit.

4.3 Step 3: Cooling

The jars must be allowed to cool down before they are sealed. This will make sure that all of your food is processed in an environment that is safe to eat. In addition, by cooling down your jars, you will ensure that they don't crack or break during processing. To speed up this process, you will want to let the jars sit in water while they cool down. You can use a little ice if you like, but let the water come up to a rolling boil before adding it.

The cooling process is very important, as it allows the jars to get a vacuum seal before you store them. Without this process, your jars could leak or split when they are filled with hot food and sealed shut.

You will want to tip the jars over to cool them off, known as a quick cooling process. The more quickly the jars cool, the faster your food will be sterilized and the less time it will take to spoil.

The temperature at which your jars are cooled must be below boiling, so you can't wait until the water boils again. If you wait too long you risk cracking and splitting your jars, which is a very expensive process to fix.

Leave the jars for about 24 hours before sealing them. It will give you plenty of time to check for air bubbles and ensure that each jar is properly sealed.

4.4 Step 4: Storing

Once you've finished canning with a water bath canner, it's important to properly store your cans to preserve the freshness of your produce. To do this, wipe them clean and remove the screw bands, then label each jar with the batch number you obtained during the canning process. You should use your jars within a year of purchase, so store them properly!

The last step to canning food is to store your jars in a cool and dry area where it will be protected from any harmful bacteria that could threaten your safety. Storing the jars properly will keep them from losing any of their original quality. You must not leave them in direct sunlight or they could heat up and spoil your food before it has finished preserving.

You also want to ensure that you don't store your jars in places where the temperature is extremely cold or hot, which will cause cracking and splitting. Therefore, you will want to keep them in a location that is between 60 and 80 degrees Fahrenheit.

This is where your home canning area will come into play. These areas should be kept in a cool and dry place, but not too humid. You need to ensure that the temperature stays no lower than 60 degrees Fahrenheit, which can be achieved with heat lamps.

Take off any screw band that you have placed on your jars. Label your jars by the number of each canning recipe you use so that you can reference them easily.

You should also write down the date they were canned and check to ensure they have been properly stored.

Jars can be kept in a cold, dry, dark place for up to a year (as recommended by National Center for Home Food Preservation).

5   WATER BATH CANNING EQUIPMENT - EVERYTHING YOU NEED TO CANNING YOUR PRODUCE

If you're a prepper, you may have heard about canning food. While this may seem like an expensive hobby, it's incredibly useful in case of disaster. Canning can preserve foods for a long time and allow you to store food away from the grocery store. Besides, you can save the harvest of your summer crops. Canning equipment is an essential tool, but there are a few more items you should have on hand. If you are a homesteader or prepper, you should consider purchasing some canning equipment. Although some people think that canning is for gardeners, it's perfect for those looking to supplement their food pantry without spending much money. Canning is the perfect solution for the never-ending grocery store shelves and preserving meats, fruits, vegetables, and pickles. Buying in bulk can also help you save money and bolster your stockpile without spending too much money. Aside from the basic canning supplies, you'll also need a few additional pieces of equipment. These supplies will help you to complete your projects faster and easier. A food mill is a great option if you plan on canning on a regular basis. Food mills have a variety of attachments and blades that make chopping vegetables faster and easier. It's worth buying one or two of these items if you want to get started with canning. Before you can start preserving your harvest, you need some basic canning equipment. Most canning kits come with plastic funnels. Stainless steel funnels are preferable. When choosing your jars, choose those that have been properly inspected. Canning kits are often available at department stores. And don't forget the lids! They're not just for home chefs - preppers use them to preserve their foods! If you're looking for inexpensive canning equipment, consider buying a pressure canner. These are relatively inexpensive, and can preserve a lot of foods for a much longer time than commercial products. They're great for preserving food - even the toughest cuts of meat! These canners can also preserve fruits, vegetables, and even meat - which is why they're such a great investment for prepper kitchens! Most canning jars, jars, and lids you need for your water bath canning are available on Amazon. You will also find that many popular brands are sold right in your home state, which means you can get them without going anywhere else. Water bath canning equipment is essential for the safe preparation of your food. Without it, you will be unable to safely sterilize your jars or seal them off so that they are sterile and sealed. You will also be unable to properly keep any pests out of your food and remove all the air introduced during the process. There are many types of canning equipment on the market and they come in various price ranges. First, you should keep all the jars and lids in good condition. Follow all manufacturers' instructions to maintain your Water Bath Canning Equipment. Also, don't forget to use food-safe gloves.

Jar Cappers

Capping jars is an essential part of the canning process, which means that it is very important that you have a jar capper in your kitchen. Without a jar capper, you will find that your jars become very hard to seal and can spill when you are working with them. This will make it much more difficult to preserve your food properly. No matter how careful you are, there is always a chance for safety risks to arise with this type of equipment.

Clean Towels

When you clean the jars after you finish the canning process, you will want to ensure that you clean them with a clean towel and not your kitchen sink. This is because when cleaning with your sink just food particles could be left on it, which could mean that they contaminate your jars and make it harder for you to preserve your food. Such can also make it more difficult for you to get a good seal on your jars.

Jars

You will have to choose which type of jar you would like to use for the canning process. Many people will choose the option of a simple mason jar, which is available in almost every grocery store in your local area. They are very inexpensive and many people already have them on hand. You will find these jars in most areas, but if you live in a very rural area, you will have to travel a little further to find them. You can also choose between pint or quart cups, which are available at almost any grocery store. You only need one type per recipe you create, ensuring you get the best produce possible.

Lids

You also should ensure you have lids for your jars. These lids will seal off the jars and keep out any pests that could contaminate your food. A good lid should fit nicely over any mason jar and provide a good seal. You will need to find another way to keep your food safe if it doesn't.

Water bath canners and pressure canners

There are two types of canning: water bath canning and pressure canning. Both methods use boiling water to process jars. Water bath canners are usually filled with at least an inch of water. On the other hand, pressure canners need more water, so you should use more water in a pressure canner than in a water bath canner. Regardless of your chosen method, you'll preserve any type of produce or meat in jars.

Canning funnels

Canning funnels come in various sizes and shapes and fit into regular or wide mouth jars. Some funnels feature graduated rims, while others are symmetrical and flat. The necks are typically long and wide and extend into the jar by different amounts. Some funnels are made of plastic or metal. Jars with a deep rim may need a narrower funnel. Purchasing jars and canning funnels is necessary to make successful water bath canning. Purchasing glass jars is a good choice as you can reuse them. Additionally, a canning funnel is important, since it keeps jar rims clean and avoids spilling. Water bath canning equipment includes a large stockpot, canning funnel, jar lifter, and measuring cups. You should also purchase a wire rack for your canner.

Cutting board

Using mason jars and screw-brand jar lifters, you can avoid the hassles of single-use lids. You can reuse these items for many years. Other items to consider buying are a food mill, cutting boards, ladles, and a stockpot. These canning supplies can be purchased at your local hardware store or online.

Knives and vegetable peelers

The knife used for vegetable peeling should be good quality, and a knife with a Y blade will be ideal for removing thick skin. Vegetable peelers also make great garnishes for desserts and cocktails.

Jar lifter and mixing bowls

Using a jar lifter is essential when water bath canning. You must lift jars from the hot water and place them on a drying rack to cool. Be extra careful to avoid tilting jars during the canning process. To keep your food fresh, follow the manufacturer's directions. After the jars cool, use the jar lifter to remove them from the canner.

Stock pot and spoons

For water bath canning, a stock pot is a must-have. These handy kitchen tools are especially useful when you need to blanch large amounts of vegetables, like broccoli or green beans. Spoons are good for several purposes like mixing.

Rack and strainers

You'll need some strainers. A good strainer can prevent the jars from touching the bottom of the canner.

Tongs and timer

Tongs and a timer are the most important tools to prepare for a successful water bath canning. If you live in a cold climate, you can use kitchen tongs or jar lifters to remove jars from boiling water. For a better grip, use rubber bands to tighten your kitchen tongs. Jar lifters are safer than ordinary kitchen tongs. And, instead of using paper towels to line your canner, use cloth towels. These are just some of the most popular canning supplies you need to get started. If you have any questions about your canning supplies or think you may need more, you should contact your local farming supply store for more information. They should be very helpful and offer you various options for whatever specific supplies you need.

6   HOW TO PRESSURE CAN IN 8 EASY STEPS

The Process of Pressure Canning consists of several steps. The first step involves heating and filling the jars. The next step is removing any air bubbles. Then, you will wipe and add the lids. Lastly, you will fill the canner to the correct level and lock the lid. It's time to can your homemade veggies or fruit. Continue reading to learn how to can different foods at home!

6.1   Step 1: Heat and Fill the Jars

To start filling the jars, heat the oven to 400 degrees Fahrenheit. Prepare a wide-mouth funnel. Place the contents in the jars, leaving about 1 inch of headspace at the top. Insert a rubber seal and ensure it fits tightly but not too tight. Leave the jars to cool in their place for several hours, ideally overnight. Then, place the lids on the jars and set them aside to cool.

To sterilize the jar lids, put them in a pot with enough water to cover them completely. Next, bring the pot to a simmer, about 180 degrees Fahrenheit. This will help prevent the lids from breaking while filling them with hot preserves. Similarly, it will reduce the chances of cracking the jars when they are filled with hot food or transferred to a boiling water bath. Once filled, the jars should be placed on a towel or wooden cutting board. Do not place them directly on a cool surface, as they may break.

Place a lid on each jar and secure it with a ring. Tighten it until the ring meets resistance. This method is known as fingertip tightening, allowing air to escape when the jars cool down. Once cool, move the jars to a cool, dark place away from the refrigerator. Remember to wash them thoroughly before storing. Otherwise, they may attract pests.

6.2   Step 2: Remove Air Bubbles

This process is called de-bubbling, and it is vitally important in the process of food processing. Insufficient headspace, or air, inside the jars will prevent the process of sealing properly and result in too much headspace and insufficient seal. Air trapped in the jars can also cause the canned product to rise above the level of the canning liquid and develop off flavors. To remove air from the jars, use heat-resistant utensils.

Using a nonmetallic spatula or a bubble freer, slide it down the side of each jar until the measuring tool is positioned at the center. Repeat this procedure two or three times around the inside of the jars. After removing the bubbles, wipe the jar rims clean with a damp paper towel. Then, place a clean lid over each jar and tighten the rim.

After filling the jars with the food of your choice, you need to remove any trapped air bubbles. You can use a bubble remover or a plastic knife to do the job. If you don't have one, you can use a jar lifter, which makes it easy to insert the jars into the canner while the lid is in the vertical position. Using a jar lifter will also prevent the jars from getting hot, resulting in burnt hands.

6.3   Step 3: Wipe and Add Lids

When pressure canning, you must ensure the lids are properly sealed and not loose. Plastic lids tend to lose a significant amount of vacuum over time and can be difficult to seal properly. The most recommended lids have two pieces, a band or ring and a flat lid bit. While you can buy reusable lids, you may want to go without them.

After sealing your jars, you should use a canner to ladle the contents into them. Make sure you leave enough headspace to avoid bubbles. Place a funnel to avoid getting food on the sides. Add the liquid, leaving at least one-fourth inch of headspace. If your jars have too much headspace, you should recheck the headspace and fill the jars again. Wipe the rims with a damp cloth to remove any air bubbles. Then screw on the lids and bands.

After the canner is finished processing, you can remove the weight and open the vent. Removing the jars from the canner is recommended if the contents are hot and steamy. If you can't lift them, use a jar lifter to transfer them to a clean surface. Afterward, store them upright and in a draft-free area for a few days to allow the contents to cool down completely.

6.4 Step 4: Fill the Canner and Lock the Lid

To make a safe, quality canned product, follow the steps below. First, fill the canner with the desired amount of liquid. To do this, place the jars in the canner one by one and lift them with a jar lifter. The lifter should be placed beneath the ring band of the lid. It is important to ensure that the jars remain upright in the canner, as tipping a jar can lead to spillage in the sealing zone. Also, use a shaped wire rack to load the jars from the upper side and lower them into the water.

After filling the canner, ensure that the vent pipe is open. Pressurize the canner at the appropriate pressure for the recipe. Once the pressure has reached zero, you may unlock the lid by detaching the weight and opening the vent. Once the timer has expired, remove the weight and jar lifter, leaving at least an inch of space between the jars. Allow the canner to cool, and then remove the jars.

6.5 Step 5: Vent the Pressure Canner

After completing the previous steps, venting the pressure canner is important to avoid overheating the food. The pressure will rise in the canner after a few minutes. You can use a weighted gauge to monitor the pressure and set a timer. When the pressure reaches the recommended pressure, the weighted gauge will start to jiggle or rattle. After the canner is vented, it's safe to leave the pressure canner on the stovetop overnight.

Next, you can remove the weight of the canner and slowly open the petcock. Wait five minutes for the pressure to reduce, and then carefully lift the lid. It's best to hold it away from your face so as not to burn yourself. If you cannot do so, the pressure canner may be too hot to handle. Once this is complete, you are ready to remove the canner's lid.

6.6 Step 6: Achieve the Correct Pressure

Before you can your food, you must achieve the correct pressure. There are different methods for achieving this pressure. Several books will tell you to remove the lid and wait for 10 minutes. Other books say to leave the lid on for at least 20 minutes. It does suggest waiting the recommended time. Regardless, you must wait for the correct pressure and temperature before removing the jars from the pot.

To ensure that the correct pressure is achieved, you should listen to the canner's weight gauge. A weighted gauge will make a rocking sound if the pressure inside is correct. Check the manual to see how often you should do this. Ideally, your canner's weight gauge will rock two to three times per minute. During the entire time, you should hear the rocking sound of the weights as the pressure builds.

6.7 Step 7: Depressurize and Open the Canner

Before you can open your pressure canner, depressurize it first. If the canner uses a vent-lock piston, depressurize it by allowing the pistons to drop back down to their normal position. If the canner has a weighted gauge, lift the weight by a few millimeters and slowly lower it. Wait until the hissing or rattle sounds stop.

Then, remove the lid of the canner. Lift the lid slowly and carefully. Once it is cool enough, place the canner on a cooling rack or towel. Avoid letting the lid sit on a cold surface or in windy conditions. You should not attempt to open the canner lid by force. It could warp and spoil the contents. Always read the manufacturer's instructions before using your pressure canner.

Before opening your pressure canner, ensure you have secured the lid and removed the weight and petcock. Heat the canner at its highest setting until the water boils and the steam flows freely. After 10 minutes, remove the weight and vent pipe. The pressure should return to zero within three to ten minutes. To do this, wait for a few minutes. It will help the canner to depressurize and open properly.

6.8 Step 8: Cool the Jars

The first step to pressure canning is to clean the jars well. Next, remove any screw bands from jars that are sealed. Wash, dry, and store the screw bands. Next, rinse the jars and label them. Include the contents of the jar, the date, and the lot number.

While pressure canning, allow the jars to cool completely before removing them from the canner. Over-packing or filling jars past the recommended headspace will blow out the liquid. This won't affect the taste or shelf life of the food. If they are hot, place a towel underneath them to catch any excess steam. Then, set the jars on a table or countertop. Ensure sufficient space between the jars to prevent them from touching.

After pressure canning, the jars should be allowed to cool to room temperature. Be sure to keep the jars separated by at least one inch. Allow them to cool for 12 to 24 hours before storing them. During this time, make sure to lift the lids of the jars carefully and do not force them. Also, be sure not to tighten the lids and do not push them too far down the center.

Before you can pressure-can your homemade jam, you must learn how to do several things. First, clean the jars. Fill them with fresh ingredients. Then, seal the lid. Keep the lid tight to trap steam. Next, build pressure to the correct altitude. Using the right pressure canner can save you time and effort. Read on to learn how to pressure-can jam safely. Then, follow these steps to make a tasty jam.

Cleaning jars

To clean jars using pressure cans, you can use a solution of 1 cup of standard white vinegar in one gallon of water. Fill the jars with the mixture and let them soak for several hours. When washing, the solution should remove the film on the jars. Aside from cleaning jars, vinegar also helps prevent the buildup of hard water on jars. Ideally, you should use vinegar to clean jars that are being reused. You should wash new jars as well. They aren't sterile when new and may have been packed in plastic wrap containing bacteria and other contaminants. Furthermore, they may have accumulated dust and small pieces of debris. Additionally, in case of breakage, glass jars may have chipped or cracked. Finally, you should avoid using pressure cans on jars that are still cold. These are likely to break or get damaged.

Filling jars

If you're considering canning, you'll want to prepare jars properly before starting the process. It's important to check the jars thoroughly before you fill them and ensure that the rims of the jars are clean before applying the lids. In addition, do not wipe the jars before they have cooled completely since this will cause a whitish film. This film is harmless, but it can interfere with the sealing of the lid. When you're ready to process, make sure the lids of your jars are fingertip-tight. You don't want air to escape during the canning process. Place your jars on a canning rack and cover them with water, preferably at least an inch deep. Bring the water to a low simmer, but don't let it boil. The time should be adjusted according to your altitude. Once the jars have reached a steady simmer, remove them from the water and allow them to stand for five minutes. Allow the jars to cool for another 12 hours.

Removing jars

To avoid spilling hot jam on your kitchen floor, you should learn to remove jars from pressure cans. You can use a heavy garbage bag to place the suspect jars in. Once the jars are cool enough to handle, you should remove the lids and place them in the regular trash can or landfill. Make sure to label the jars and store them away from direct light.

After processing your jars in a pressure can, you must leave them for five to 10 minutes. The longer you leave them, the more likely they are to leak. Make sure the seals are finger-tight to prevent liquid from escaping. If they aren't, don't force them. It might cause them to pop open. If this happens, you should allow the jars to rest at room temperature for ten minutes before removing them from the pressure can.

7 PRESSURE CANNING EQUIPMENT

There are several things you must have to pressure can foods. The pressure canner, Canning Jars, Lids and Rings, and Tongs are just a few. But if you plan to can meat, fish, vegetables, and fruits, you'll also need a few other items. Below, we'll discuss what you must have. And don't forget to get the requisite tools.

The tools and equipment you need to begin pressure canning include a food mill for finely grinding your ingredients, a scale for measuring precisely, and a magnetic lid lifter. Many home canners use these items to easily place lids on jars. Therefore, most home canners already own these items. Other essentials include an oven mitt to protect your hands from the heat of the process, tongs for picking up hot items, and a colander for rinsing fresh fruits and vegetables.

A Pressure Canner

To successfully can foods in a pressure canner, it is crucial to follow the manufacturer's instructions. In addition, certain foods cannot be pressure canned in boiling water, such as tomatoes and unpickled vegetables.

The canner should be heated to the maximum recommended pressure for your geographic altitude. When the pressure is too low, adjust the heat. To ensure constant pressure, jiggle the weighted gauge several times a minute or rock slowly. Loss of pressure may cause underprocessing. Large pressure fluctuations may also cause liquid to drain out of jars. To avoid these risks, try to maintain a steady pressure throughout the entire process.

After determining the type of food to process, prepare the pressure canner. It must be able to process foods with a pH level over 4.6. Low-acid foods include vegetables, meat sauces, and soups. Once the pressure gauge is at the recommended pressure, add the weights. The pressure will build for three to 10 minutes. When the pressure gauge indicates zero, remove the weights.

Canning Jars

Before you begin pressure canning, you must understand the tools to ensure a successful batch of home canned goods. A jar lifter is a useful tool that will allow you to carefully lift jars from boiling water. It is similar to a pair of tongs, but its notched end is made for lifting hot jars. A stainless steel scoop helps guide food into the jar.

There are different kinds of jars to choose from, but they are all essential for the canning process. There are wide-mouth jars, regular-mouth jars, and Tupperware. Wide-mouth jars are ideal for pickles and larger quantities of jam, while regular-mouth jars are generally more versatile and are great for sauces and jams.

To ensure a safe canning process, get a complete canning kit. This set includes six essential tools: a jar lifter, wide-mouth funnel, bubble popper, headspace measurer, and magnetic lid lifter. In addition, tongs are useful for packing food, while a jar wrench makes jar rings finger-tight.

Lids and Rings

Before you start canning, you should prepare the jars and lids for the process. For best results, preheat the jars and lids before you begin. To ensure proper sealing, use the proper lid that allows the jar to expand, has a clean vent, and is finger-tight. Do not re-use the lids and rings after the first use. After the first use, the sealing compound will have indented and not produce an airtight seal. Moreover, you should also test the packaging components for their suitability.

If you purchase your lids online, check the website's information to ensure you are not dealing with a scammer. Also, ensure that the website offers a clear return policy and clear copy. You can also buy lids that come with bands. The screw bands are recyclable. For additional convenience, you can also purchase flat lids, if you prefer that. They come in various shapes and colors and can be used for several types of canning projects.

Tongs

Modern canning tongs are designed to make jar lifting easier and safer, with a textured non-slip gripper edge to help remove jars safely from boiling water. They also have a curved handle for a firm ergonomic grip. They are made from stainless steel or plastic. For pressure canning, you can use kitchen tongs, but getting a set designed specifically for this process is important.

When it comes to canning, you can't do it without the proper tools. Pressure canners have everything you need to sterilize your canned food, including the jars. In addition, a set of tongs helps you keep your hands safe while handling hot water, as long as the seal is good. Tongs are also essential when handling chunky things such as beans, jam, or other foods.

Jar Lifter

A Jar Lifter for pressure canning is an attachment that will enable you to properly handle a large canning jar. It is designed with two loops on either end of a continuous strip of resilient material. One loop is positioned at the wide mouth and extends downward as rails, while the other is placed externally. Both loops are designed to fit over a large canning jar, and the lifter has loops that can be operated manually or automatically.

The tongs of a jar lifter fit snugly around the mouth of a regular-sized canning jar and have complete loop grippers for easy guidance over the neck of the desired jar. Once the loops are fully wrapped around the neck of the jar, it won't fall off, and you can use it to remove the water from a sterilized jar. Unlike other canning tools, the jar lifter is designed to hold a hot jar.

Canning Funnel

Several types of canning funnels are available. Some are made of plastic, while others of metal. Some have graduated stepped necks, while others have a flat, sloping rim. Some are dishwasher-safe, while others are made for use in narrow-mouth jars. While not every jar size requires a particular funnel, some have more than one.

A canning funnel is an essential tool for the canning process. Using a clean rim to create a good lid-to-jar seal is crucial. The basic canning funnel is adequate, but you should consider upgrading to a double-walled one for increased safety. The Prepworks model from Progressive has a double-walled design and extendable outer wall. A measuring device on the outer rim can help you avoid overfilling the jar.

Other essential canning tools include jar lifters and food scales. A jar lifter is a pair of tongs with rubberized ends that fit tightly around canning jars. These tools will save you from burnt fingers while you're canning. Most home canners will already have most of these items. In addition to jar lifters, you may want to invest in an oven mitt and tongs.

A chopstick or stir stick

A chopstick or stir stick is a must-have if you live above a certain elevation. These small blunt utensils are essential for pressure canning because they press the pickled food and force out air bubbles. Chopsticks and stir sticks are readily available in most kitchen drawers. A timer is also helpful for keeping track of the cooking time.

When starting pressure canning, leave adequate headspace between the food and the lid. Read the recipe carefully and include the appropriate amount of headspace for your product. For most foods, 1 inch of headspace is ideal, while a half-inch is fine for acidic foods like tomatoes and pickles. For fruit and juices, it is best to leave 1/4-inch headspace. Before you begin canning, remove any air bubbles by gently stirring the contents using a chopstick or knife. Make sure to wipe the rim of the jar clean. After the jar has been properly prepared, set the lid in place and tighten the band until it resists.

A Stockpot or Dutch Oven

A Stockpot or Dutch Oven is an essential piece of home canning equipment. While a Dutch oven is much more versatile than a stock pot, it is heavier and less portable. A stockpot is better suited for cooking large quantities of food in one pot. But a Dutch oven becomes more appropriate if you need a larger volume of food to can.

A stockpot is the most suitable pressure canning utensil if you plan to make large batches of sauce or stock. It also makes it easy to drain. Dutch ovens are heavy cast iron pots with a tight-fitting lid. They are great for making a large amount of food and can be used to make larger batches of food. A Dutch Oven can also be used for preserving food in jars.

The shape is the primary difference between a stock pot and a Dutch oven. A Dutch oven is an oval or circular pot with sloping sides. The lid is tight-fitting, while a stock pot is wider and taller. The Dutch oven can be used in an oven, but it takes longer to heat up and maintain a constant temperature.

A Kitchen Timer

If you are a pressure canner, a kitchen timer is an essential piece of equipment. In addition, pressure canning requires a high-quality pressure cooker and a dial gauge that must be checked at least once a year. You can find a testing service near you or contact the manufacturer for more information. Purchasing a new pressure canner and jars is the best option, but you may use your old ones in the meantime.

When pressure canning, the canner should be brought to the specified pressure within three to ten minutes. You can check this by the sound of the pressure regulator or by the needle on the dial gauge. Once the pressure is reached, set the timer for the appropriate amount of time to process the food. If pressure drops, reset the timer for the required processing time. A kitchen timer will also help you avoid rushing the process.

A Slotted Spoon

This is a cooking equipment with openings to allow the liquid to pass through while preserving larger solids on the top. A slotted spoon is useful for transferring the fruit from the canner to the jar. Packing the fruit tightly can prevent air bubbles and help prevent the food from being overly compressed. Adding liquid to jars with whole fruit will require approximately 3/4 inch of headspace. For jam and preserves, leaving about 1/2-inch of headspace will be sufficient. However, leaving too much headspace can cause the food to discolor.

Cheesecloth or Strainer

Cheesecloth is a cotton cloth that is commonly used for food preparation. You can also use other cotton fabrics like a flour sack towel or a clean, dry pillowcase. Stockings or tights are another alternative, but be sure to wash them well before you use them. When using a cloth, liquids must have enough time to pass through the cloth before the food is safe.

If you don't want to buy a strainer, you can make your own. Simply place the herbs into the cheesecloth and tie them with twine. You can also tie loose tea leaves together with cheesecloth. The cheesecloth also serves as a gauze. If you cut yourself or get a wound, immediately wash it with soap and apply an antibacterial cream. Then cover it with a piece of clean, unused cheesecloth to prevent infection.

7.1 How to Choose the Suitable Pressure Canner

If you have a garden, you must know how to choose a suitable pressure canner. For example, if your garden produces too much, you might need a pressure canner with a larger capacity to keep the surplus of produce in one place. On the other hand, if you don't have enough freezer space, you could get a small pressure canner and use it to store the excess food in the freezer. Or, perhaps you have an apple tree that needs some serious maintenance but don't know where to find one.

Cost

Purchasing a pressure canner may seem expensive, but the best ones are worth every penny. The Presto brand has some affordable pressure canners. The Presto 01784 model, for example, costs around $120 and performs just as well as more expensive models. And unlike its competitors, it has an induction-compatible stainless steel bottom for even faster heating. So the price is a good indicator of how well the pressure canner will last.

When it comes to cost, a pressure canner costs $100 to $500, depending on its size. The jars are very durable and can be used for years. However, you should be sure to buy a set of jars, lids, and accessories. In addition to a pressure canner, you may also need jars, clean kitchen towels, potholders, and a digital timer. Purchasing an accessory like a magnetic lid lifter will also help you avoid accidents during the canning process.

Capacity

The capacity of a pressure canner is a key consideration when purchasing one. A pressure canner is designed to produce enough food to fill a quart-sized jar. The higher the capacity, the larger the jar should be. In addition to size, you should consider how much food you'll prepare. A pressure canner is heavy when fully loaded. Make sure the handles are heat-resistant.

A safety feature is a weighted gauge. A weighted gauge, sometimes called a dead-weight gauge, controls the pressure inside the canner. It allows steam to build to the proper pressure while releasing excess steam. This gauge is noisy, but it is accurate. One downside to the weighted gauge is that it doesn't accurately measure pressure at high altitudes. So while it is very convenient, it's also more expensive.

Material

There are several advantages to purchasing a high-quality pressure canner. A properly designed pressure canner will last a lifetime. The first is its ease of use. The handles of pressure canners should have a large, comfortable grip and be made from heat-resistant materials. The knobs should also be of heat-resistant material. The final benefit is that a high-quality pressure canner will be sturdy, and you won't need to worry about your canner falling apart.

A certified pressure canner is safer than a pressure cooker because it does not require sterilization of boiling water. The operating mechanism is also important. It should have a capacity listed on the label. Pressure canners come in different capacities, and the number is usually listed in quarts. Make sure you choose a high-quality pressure canner based on its capacity. You may want to purchase a smaller pressure canner for your first attempt. Make sure to buy a high-quality pressure canner with a capacity of at least nine pints or seven quarts.

8 SAFETY IN CANNING AND PRESERVING

8.1 Safety Tips for Water Bath Canning

If you're a prepper, a homesteader, or someone just interested in preparing for the future, you should learn how to can. This skill will help you save money, while helping you have your food supply. While pressure canners are great for high-acid foods, water bath canning is safer for low-acid foods. To avoid tainting food by bacteria, you must boil your jars and lids for 10 minutes. The jars don't need rings, however.

It's always safer to can your food. Not only is it cheaper than buying food, but it also provides the nutrients your family needs to stay healthy and strong. You'll also have plenty of food to choose from if you're in a pinch. Plus, canning can help you take advantage of sales and discounts. Such can also help you save money on the cost of vegetables, fruits, and meats.

After processing your food, inspect the containers to make sure they're clean and free of damage. Check the jars for a tight seal. Make sure they're not broken or smashed. A broken jar can ruin the food you've preserved. In addition, you should disinfect jars, lids, and bands with boiling water. Then, place them in a water bath canner.

You need a boiling water bath canner. A boiling water bath canner comes in many varieties. You can also use a large pot for your canning needs. Be sure it holds at least 21 quarts of water. It should also contain a canning rack and enough head room to keep water at a rolling boil. The water should cover the jars by one to two inches.

Properly acidifying your canned goods is crucial to their safety. Proper pickling techniques ensure that food is acidic enough to withstand water baths. Make sure you use a high-quality vinegar to do the job right the first time. Using vinegar with low acidity will kill bacteria. If you're worried about the acidity of your foods, you can use pressure canning, which is a safer method for preserving some foods.

8.2 Errors to Avoid

When water bath canning, there are some common mistakes to watch out for. These mistakes can cause your cans to buckle or seal improperly. Be sure to keep the lids fingertip tight. The water bath takes care of this problem. Keeping these mistakes in mind will ensure that your canning experience is as hassle-free as possible. Read on to learn more about these mistakes and avoid them.

While some of these mistakes are harmless, they can compromise the safety of your food. For example, you should not can baked goods like cakes and breads. While canning kills some bacteria, it does not destroy the organism that causes botulism. Incorrectly sealing jars can result in spoilage or even death. Here are five common mistakes to avoid.

Before you begin canning, ensure the jars are clean and debris-free. Always wipe the jars' rims before placing them in the canner. Don't wipe jars before cooling them - this can result in a spilled or broken jar. Incorrect jar placement also affects sealing. Always leave a gap of at least two inches between the lid and the jar. The correct amount of water is important for pressure and water bath canning. Water bath canners require 1 to 2 inches of water to cover the jar tops. While some water will evaporate during the process, you need to add another 2 inches to ensure that your food is evenly heated and killed all pathogens. Incorrect water temperature may result in jars with bubbles. Do not overfill jars.Leaving jars in a water bath canner overnight can lead to seal failure. If the lid is left on while the food is cooling, it promotes siphoning. Siphoning of liquid can push the food out of the jar and cause it to get dirty. Another risk of premature jar removal is improper lid tampering, another common mistake. Leaving jars in a water bath canner overnight is also not recommended. Preserves that do not set or are too runny result from incorrect directions. A few minutes more may be needed to reach jelling or boiling point. If you do not have time to cook them longer, try heating them to the jelling point. In case of jam, the first jar should slide easily off a spoon in a sheet, not drip. After that, ladle the unset preserves into jars and cover them with a previously heated lid. If the jam does not set, re-process your preserves as per the original recipe. A false seal occurs when the lids of the jars indent after cooling. Without a lid, the liquids cannot reach the proper temperature to seal. Unless the lids are completely sealed, they will eventually leak. As a result, the food inside the jars will spoil without you knowing. False seals are difficult to detect from outside, because they will look indented on the outside, but will not release when tested with a finger.

Over-tightening lids

Using a pressure canner or water bath canner is essential for sealing the jars. It is also vital to avoid over-tightening the lids of your jars. Over-tightening your lids can result in a faulty seal and a funky-looking jar. A proper amount of twist is one fingertip tight. To avoid over-tightening your lids, mark them with a marker. Do not crank down the bands. Using metal tools could ruin the jars.

Over-heating

If you're thinking of canning your food, you might wonder whether or not you should use water bath canning. There are several ways to use the process, and water bath canning is one of them. Fruits and vegetables high in acidity are best canned in this way. You can also try filling your jars with raw produce or a cold pack. It's up to you, but most producers recommend using a water bath canning method if you're planning on canning a specific type of produce.

Adding thickener

You might need to add a thickener while water bath canning for several reasons. For starters, thickeners are not always natural. Some are just plain bad for you. There are several different types. Here are three common examples of things you can do to avoid using them:

Over-tightening rings

When canning, avoid over-tightening the rings on your jars. If they're too tight, air won't escape, and the lid will warp or distort. Also, too-tight bands might not create a vacuum seal. Instead, the rings should be snug to the touch, but not too loose that they'll slip off the jar.

Oozing out of jars

When preparing foods for canning, the main aim is to avoid oozing out of the jars. This problem can occur for several reasons, from a lack of water in a boiling water bath canner to the packed nature of the food. Either way, you'll need to remove air bubbles to avoid this problem. Also, make sure to use the recommended headspace when canning.

8.3 Principles of Food Conservation in Water Bath Canning

The basic principle of food conservation in water bath canning is to put sealed containers in boiling water. The amount of water needed to cover the jars depends on the food product you're preserving. The boiling water around the jars never reaches 100 degrees Celsius. Therefore, water bath canning is a safer way to preserve food than pressure canning. Read on to learn how to preserve food in a water bath. First, clean your food thoroughly. Dirt contains bacteria that are hard to kill, so soaking foods for a long time will reduce their flavor and nutrients. Always wash your produce thoroughly before processing it. Fruits and vegetables are often packed raw, while others are cooked and packed with a hot pack. While some fruits and vegetables are compatible with either method, hot packing generally gives them a better color and taste. The basic principles of food conservation in water bath canning involve using a hermetically sealed container and applying a high temperature to destroy spoilage organisms. This process also protects the nutritional and physical quality of the food. There are many ways to can food, but the process is similar for all types of containers. Metal cans are the most common type, but there are also glass jars and retort pouches. You need a wide mouth funnel, measuring cups, and a boiling pot to use a water bath canner. You can buy a boiling water bath canner or make one using existing equipment. Make sure to use a canner with a deep enough reservoir to place your rack in it. You also need to purchase jars and clean them properly. This is not a complicated process, but following the canning recipe carefully and using a high-quality water bath canner is important. The process of canning is a safe and efficient way to preserve foods. Foods are placed in jars and heated to a precise temperature. This process destroys harmful microorganisms and inactivates enzymes that would otherwise cause food to spoil. In addition, the process creates a vacuum seal and preserves food quality when properly done. The process is also inexpensive. As a result, this method is very popular and has many benefits. Once you've filled your jars, fill the canner to the appropriate height. When filling, leave about an inch of water between the jars to prevent breakage. When filling the canner, turn the heat setting to the highest setting. Ensure the water boils slowly and steadily until it reaches the desired boiling point. You may also want to adjust the heat level if the water doesn't boil.

8.4 Jar Sterilizations in Water Bath Canning

The process of jar sterilization is very simple. First, fill a deep pot with water and place your canner in it. Next, cover the jars with hot tap water. Place them on a medium heat, and simmer for 10 minutes. Remove the lids and rings with tongs when the water is hot enough. Once sterilized, you can fill the jars and process them. The National Center for Home Food Preparation has specific recommendations for jar sterilization. If a recipe specifies five to 10 minutes, omit the jar sterilization step. While jar sterilization is unnecessary for jellied products, it requires additional energy and time. In addition, jar sterilization is unnecessary at high altitudes because the boiling water process time is sufficient to kill bacterial growth. Before 1970, boiling was a requirement. Jars with metal lids were typically used as containers in home-canned goods. However, boiling the lids was not a good practice, as this can lead to broken seals and potentially contaminated food. Instead, experts recommend placing the lids in a water bath canner with a rack. The jars should be filled with about an inch of water. After the food is ready for canning, sterilize the jars using a wide-mouth funnel. When filling the jars, leave about a 1/4-inch head space. When you are using a funnel, be sure to use a rubber spatula to remove air bubbles. After sterilization, the jars should be fingertip tight. Once the jars are filled, you can begin packing them into the canner. Preparing your canner is an important step in the canning process. If you are using a dishwasher, use the "sanitize" setting, which will heat water to 150 degrees Fahrenheit. If you don't have electricity, use a wood or grill to sterilize your jars. If you're uncomfortable using electricity, sterilizing jars in a water bath is a great alternative to boiling. Before sterilizing your jars, ensure that your canning surface is clean. It can harbor bacteria if you're using bare countertops and dish towels. Also, avoid adding hot or cold food to old jars. This can result in damage and spoilage. So make sure to clean everything thoroughly before sterilizing. Finally, there are a couple of things to remember about jar sterilization. Before using jars for water bath canning, make sure they're clean. Using hot water with soap will clean and sterilize jars, and the lids should also be clean. To ensure a safe seal, use new lids for jars each time you can food. Once you're done, you'll be ready to start your water bath canning! After jar sterilization, it's time to store your canned food. You can reuse jars if the lid doesn't seal. Just make sure to remove any screw bands and wipe them clean. When you're done with your canning, store them in a cool, dry place, and use them within a year. Just remember to keep them properly labeled. And remember, if you're unsure what to label, you should check for nicks and scuffs.

8.5 Summary of Safety Tips for Water Bath Canning

- Fill the water bath canner no higher than the level of the canning jars. the lids of the canning jars should always be higher than the water level. If necessary, add extra water.

- If you're putting newly cooked hot food into canning jars, ensure the jars are also hot.

- Ensure that your canning jars and lids have been thoroughly cleaned and sterilized.

- Lower the canning jars into the hot water bath using a jar lifter.

- Put on gloves while handling the lifter

- Put on gloves while handling the canning jars when hot

- Always leave one inch of headspace above the meal before sealing the lid finger-tight.

- Store canned water bath items away from direct heat.

9 FAQs

If you have been thinking about preserving food, you might be wondering about some of the commonly asked questions regarding water bath canning. These are things like Can you bake bread or cake in a canning jar? Can you can applesauce, pickles, or other items? If you aren't sure how to prepare food for water bath canning, don't worry - there are answers to all these questions!

Do's And Don'ts

Canning is simple, but you must follow our instructions carefully because it can result in disastrous consequences.

- Never eat food if you suspect that it has gone bad. Just throw it away. Home-canned food can rot for several reasons. They include a crack in a jar, insufficient cooking time, and a dent in the lid. If you ever notice any of these signs, never taste them.
- Never put fat or butter into your home-canned products because they slow heat transfer during the boiling process and will decrease food's life.
- Never add more spices than the recipe requires because it could be unsafe.
- Read carefully all the recipes because you have to know what to do and be organized.
- Never use overripe food for canning.

Can I use my Own Recipes When Canning?

Canning can be a fun and exciting process. You can change the basic recipe to suit your taste in terms of ingredients, spices or seasonings, or enhance the end product by adding a special ingredient that appeals to you. For example, you can add fruit juices or different forms of sweeteners that enhance the taste even further. However, canned foods made from scratch with your recipes do not have the same shelf life as recipes that are commercially produced for sale in stores.

Can I use mixed jar sizes or mixed foods in the same batch?

Jars are used to hold food during canning. A jar that is slightly smaller than the food can be used, but if it is smooshed in the process and gets damaged, it cannot be reused. Do not fill a jar more than three-quarters full. The recipe should be for that size jar, so it will fit in the canner.

How do I safely can my tomato sauce with a pressure canner or water bath canning?

Tomatoes sauces are cooked during the canning process using a water bath. You can also use a pressure cooker, which is usually used for much higher temperatures. A pressure cooker makes saucy foods normally cooked in a sauce or gravy. The tomato sauce is reduced by simmering the tomatoes during the water bath process or using a slow cooker during the pressure canning process to create a smooth finished product that is tasty and retains its original red color.

How long do you keep food with pressure or water bath canning?

The USDA recommends that you follow the recipe's instructions and keep the food in your pantry for a minimum of one year. In addition, it is recommended that you check the jar periodically and release any air bubbles as they appear. Finally, if mold or bacteria appear, do not consume the food and throw it out, even if you have not opened the jar.

What if a canning jar does NOT seal?

Since canning jars are used the same way as water jugs and food storage containers, they contain the same amount of bacteria. These bacteria may enter your food when you open the jar. Once the seal is broken, it will be a few hours before it is safe to eat.

If your jar does not seal perfectly, you should discard the product and start with a new batch.

Please remember that once you open a jar, you need to refrigerate it immediately.

What foods should NOT be canned?

Do not place food in your pressure canner or water bath canning jars that have been frozen. This can cause a jar to explode, making you an orphan.

Do not use the sterilizing process for food in your pressure canner or water bath on items that contain raw meat, fish, poultry, eggs, or dairy products. Raw meat and poultry may be contaminated with bacteria such as Salmonella and E.coli. In addition, eggs may contain Salmonella and E. coli before they are cooked.

How to avoid the proliferation of bacteria?

Keep your jars and containers clean from any dust or built-up residue. Wash them in hot, soapy water and scrub them vigorously with a brush. Using a small amount of bleach solution to wash your jars will also help kill any bacterial spores that may be present.

Can you bake bread or cake in a canning jar?

Yes, but not a loaf. A cake or bread baked in a canning jar is unlikely to have a long shelf life and will lose its texture after a few months. This problem can be solved by using a long-life baking solution. This method has been around for centuries and is still popular for home cooks. A cake can last as long as six months, depending on the recipe and the storage temperature.

Unfortunately, there are several reasons why home canning jars may not be suitable for baking bread and cake. First, many cake recipes lack acid, meaning a high pH level will be created in the jar. At this pH level, bacteria can grow and cause a potentially deadly food borne illness. Baking cakes and quick breads in jars can also introduce a bacterium known as Clostridium botulinum, which is deadly if ingested.

Once you've baked the batter, pour it into the prepared jars. Fill the jars about half way full with batter. Wipe the rims well before filling them with batter. Bake the cakes for about 35 to 45 minutes, or until a toothpick inserted in the middle comes out clean. You can then put hot rings and seals on the jars. The cake batter will keep well for several months without refrigeration.

Can you can applesauce in a water bath canner?

If you can canning, you'll want to make sure you're using the proper canning equipment. You will need a large stock pot or water bath canner, a food mill, and two large bowls. Then, you will need a food mill or a vegetable strainer. You should also peel the apples and prepare them for processing. Here's how to do it.

Before starting your canning project, you should measure the amount of applesauce you will make. Remember, canned applesauce can cause a sticky mess in the canner. Moreover, it will make your jars impossible to seal. The main reason for this is that applesauce tends to contain air. When it's pureed, it introduces additional air. To drive out most of that air, you should bring the applesauce to a boil and keep it simmering for 10 minutes.

You can add dried spices to your applesauce to make it more tasty. You can also add lemon juice to the apples to brighten the flavor and color. Lastly, you can add some sugar or honey to make it sweeter. You should make sure the headspace in the jars is at least 1/2 inch, since it's crucial for proper processing. Besides, you can also add a lid to your jars to prevent bubbles.

Can you can pickles in a water bath canner?

If so, how long should you can them for? The answer depends on how long you will wait for your jars to cool before you check them. The jars will have a slight concave shape due to the vacuum created during the process. If they don't seal properly, it is best to check them again the next morning.

After you have canned your pickles, it is a good idea to keep them in the refrigerator for a month or year. Check them for bad seals and other warning signs. For example, they might have a bulging lid, a change in color or brine, or they might smell funny. Make sure you eat the pickles within three months or you may be stuck with a bad batch.

If you're just getting started with canning, you can choose a simple five-pint recipe for your first batch. A five-pint jar can produce crisp, flavorful pickles, even for the novice. First, prepare the jars. The brine is made by boiling four cups of water, four cups of vinegar, and half a cup of salt.

What is water bath canning?

Water bath canning is the process of sealing in your food using a large pot filled with boiling water. The jars are placed inside the pot and are completely submerged under the boiling water. This creates a large amount of steam, which will cause them to be sterilized just as they would be if you had used an oven. This is the preferred method for canning in the United States because it provides a safe way to keep your food protected from any germs inside it.

How long does it take to water bath can?

The amount of time it takes to water bath will depend on the type and size of your jars. If you are working with small jars and only one recipe, you can get them canned in just a few hours. On the other hand, if you are working with large jars and many recipes, then it could take you an entire day to get all of your food preserved.

The length of time will also depend on how long it takes to sterilize the jars. After submerging in the boiling water for a while, they should handle the pressure applied to them when you place the lid on them. If they don't, you will need to let them sit for a little longer.

How is water bath canning different from pressure canning?

The way the food is preserved is completely different between water bath canning and pressure canning. With pressure canning, the jars are placed in a sealed box that locks in humidity. It means that it will keep out any bacteria and mold from getting into your food. When you use water bath canning, you will find that the jars are exposed to bacteria, but they are sterilized by a combination of boiling water and the pressure placed on them by the lid. So it allows them to keep their food safe without worrying about it getting spoiled.

Can you reuse canning water?

This is a very good question, because one of the main reasons people don't want to water bath can is that they don't want to go through the time and expense of boiling it. However, if you have already used your jars before and sealed them off, you may reuse this water for your next batch. Just make sure you completely clean the jars before opening them and lay a new batch of your food inside them. Then, when you take this route, you can still enjoy the convenience of water bath canning and not worry about the extra time and expense.

Is it possible to replace the liquid loose during the process?

This is another great question about the water bath canning process. If you use a recipe with a lot of liquid inside, ensure that you don't overfill your jars. You won't replace any liquid lost during the process, because this will reduce the pressure applied to the food and make it easier for bacteria to get in. However, if you use a recipe with little liquid, you can use the entire amount of water.

Do I need to completely fill my jars?

This is another great question about the water bath canning process. Why would you want to take away half of your jars when you go through the trouble of doing this? If they are not filled up, they won't hold their weight and may not seal properly. They may also leak when heated up and the food will end up draining out. They will also take longer to sterilize, which could lead to the food spoiling before you get the chance to open it. On the other hand, if they are full and there is no extra room in any of them, they may not seal properly and your food could spoil. For this reason, it is best to use a recipe with enough liquid and put one or two extra inches of liquid inside your jars.

What is the durability of canned food?

If you have done your job and sealed your jars properly, you can enjoy eating your canned food for up to three years. It may not be shipped to you straight from the distributor, but it should remain safe and nutritious when it reaches you if it is shipped well. You can even keep it in the pantry for up to five years, making this a great way of preserving food that doesn't need to be eaten immediately. This is great for items you want to add to your stockpile of food, but you don't always have the time or energy to do it.

What are the health benefits of water bath canning?

The reason that people love using water bath canning is because it kills off any harmful bacteria and spores at the same time. This doesn't just make it safe for you to eat but also keeps your food as fresh as possible when you open them. You will also notice that it can remove many unnecessary additives from your food, so you won't have to worry about eating preservatives. It can also help to increase the shelf life of your food if it is properly sealed, making it easy for you to use when you need it.

Can you use a pressure cooker instead of a boiling water bath?

Yes, you can use a pressure cooker instead of a boiling water bath, as long as it is specially designed for canning. These pressure cookers will be able to regulate the temperature and pressure so you don't have to worry about changing it while preserving your food. In addition, if you do this, the process will go smoother and faster than if you were using your regular pressure cooker for this purpose. There are also many other benefits to this method instead of boiling water.

Are certain times of the year better for canning?

Yes, you should only try to preserve your food during the warmer months of the year when it is hot and humid. It will help kill off bacteria and mold spores that may try to jump on your food. You should also try to ensure it is sealed, as this will help keep out any other airborne germs that may try to get in. It would also be a good idea to destroy the mold spores if you can see them, as these are very dangerous for your health.

Are there any chemicals that need to be added to the water?

No, you don't have to add chemicals when using water bath canning. However, you should always ensure that your water is clean and clear from other minerals or additives. You would only need to do this if the water isn't healthy for your food. For example, you should never add chlorine or bleach to your canned food because it will destroy all its vitamins and nutrients.

When do you add the sugar to the jars?

You don't need to add any sugar to your jars when you are canning, unless you are making a sweet or marmalade fruit. You would only need to add it if you have added a lot of extra water, which will make your food too sweet. However, as long as your food is perfectly preserved, it won't be an issue for most people.

Why do canning jars break in water bath?

This will all come down to the condition of your jar. If it is too old or has been used for other purposes, it may not handle the heat of a water bath. Also, you should use a perfectly clean jar each time you go through this process, as any impurities could cause your jar to break.

What is the correct way of filling jars?

When filling your jars for water bath canning, you must ensure that you fill them up to the shoulder. The shoulder is the point at which it is so full that there is no extra room and it won't seal properly. However, there are other parts of a jar than the shoulder, so ensure you don't fill them up completely full.

What will happen if lids don't pop when canning?

If your lids don't pop when you are canning, then this could be a sign that they have gone bad. You may also notice that the jars are going soft and getting moldy. It will also be very difficult to get the air out of them; they may explode if you put them in the pressure cooker. This will ruin your cans and make a huge mess, so try to avoid it whenever possible.

How do you know that the seal is good?

The easiest way to know that the seal is good is to see the lid pop. If you are using a glass jar, you should see it because light enters the jar and acts as a sealant. You can also hear it when you hold your jar and ensure that there is no air inside it. However, if you use an aluminum jar, you will use your ears because these jars don't give off any sound.

How can you tell if canned food has botulism?

There are some signs that an illness could be botulism, which include a general feeling of sickness, diarrhea, and a generally runny nose. You could also notice that your food looks very plastic and moldy and the jars look very faded. If you want to ensure that it isn't botulism, you should throw the rest of your can in the trash.

Can you reprocess jars that didn't seal?

Yes, you can reprocess jars that didn't seal. Because they are in a sealed state and they are still made of the same material, then this means that they will go through the sealing process again. Ensure that your jars are clean and dry before you do this. It is a good way to eliminate any extra air left in them or moldy spots on them.

What's a false seal in canning?

False seals in canning occur when the lid is not properly placed over the container. This can cause it to burst or explode when it is being heated. It could also cause a metal seal regardless of the lid being on it too tightly, which will cause the metal to rust or corrode.

Can homemade baby food be canned?

Yes, you can easily can homemade baby food. This allows you to preserve your baby's food and feed it to them whenever you need. It will also help them to develop a taste for the different flavors and textures, which is especially important for infants.

Why do some lids fail to seal?

If your lids fail to seal, this can happen for several reasons. You should always ensure that you are using canning jars made for use in the water bath canning process. They will have a special sealant around them to help with their sealing process, so they won't leak at all. It is also important to put the lid on properly and not make it too tight or loose on the jar.

Is food poisonous if it sits in a sealed jar for months?

Food that sits in a sealed jar is never poisonous, as long as you use the water bath canning process. This process will seal the lid and vacuum your jars, which means they are completely air tight. If your food hasn't been preserved properly, you must throw them away immediately.

What can I use to make homemade baby food?

You can make homemade baby food with several different ingredients. This is an easy and cost-effective way to stock up on your family's tools, food, and containers. You can buy jars in different sizes, from pint to quart, and there are also many ways to make your cookie dough into lotion or soup.

10 WATER BATH CANNING RECIPES

10.1 MARMALADES

10.1.1 Zucchini Marmalade

Serves: 12-pint jars | Preparation time: 10 mins | Cooking Time: 15 mins

Ingredients:

- Zucchini, shredded - 4 c.
- Sugar - 5 c.
- Peeled, deseeded, and sliced orange - 1

Procedure:

1. Using your blender, process the orange segments and orange peel for 2 minutes.
2. Next, add zucchini, sugar, and orange in a saucepan, then boil for 15 minutes.
3. Finally, allow it to cool.
4. You can serve or store it for later,

Nutrition per serving: Calories 326 | Fat 0.1 g | Carbs 86.4 g | Sugar 85.4 g | Protein 0.6 g | Potassium 0 mg

10.1.2 Onion Marmalade

Serves: 4-pint jars | Preparation Time: 10 mins | Cooking Time: 25 mins

Ingredients:

- Sliced onions - 2
- Salt - ¼ tsp.
- Sugar - 1 tsp.
- Red wine vinegar - 1 tbsp.
- Red wine - 1/3 c.
- Olive oil - ¼ c.

Procedure:

1. Warm oil in a saucepan.
2. Next, add the onion, then cook for 15 minutes.
3. Add sugar, then continue cooking for additional 5 minutes. Next, pour in wine, then cook for 10 minutes.

4. Pull from the heat, then add vinegar and salt. Finally, stir to mix.
5. You can store or serve.

Nutrition per serving: Calories 159 | Fat 12.7 g | Carbs 8.6 g | Sugar 4.4 g | Protein 0.8 g | Potassium 0 mg

10.1.3 Orange Marmalade

Serves: 6-pint jars | Preparation time: 10 mins | Cooking Time: 45 mins

Ingredients:

- Water - 1 c.
- Thinly sliced oranges - 1 lb.
- Sugar - 1 c.
- Vanilla extract - 1 tsp.

Procedure:

1. Add oranges and the other ingredients into a saucepan. Next, boil the mixture, then simmer for 40 minutes after reducing the heat.
2. Finally, let it cool.
3. You can serve or store it for later.

Nutrition per serving: Calories 163 | Fat 0.1 g | Carbs 42.3 g | Sugar 40.5 g | Protein 0.7 g

10.1.4 Rhubarb Raisin Marmalade

Serves: 4-pint jars | Preparation time: 35 mins | Cooking Time: 20 mins

Ingredients:

- Sugar - 6 c.
- Diced rhubarb - 6 c.
- Lemon, zest & juice - 1
- Oranges, zest & juice - 2
- Raisins - 1 c.
- Strawberries - 1½ c.
- Salt – ¼ tsp.

Procedure:

1. In your pot, add the ingredients except for raisins. Continue cooking the mixture until the sugar gets to dissolve.
2. Next, add the raisins, boil, then cook for 5 minutes.
3. In sterilized hot jars, pour the marmalade, and leave ½" space above. Cover with the lid.
4. Finally, boil your jars for 10 minutes in a water bath.
5. You can serve or store it for later after cooling.

Nutrition per serving: Calories 168 | Fat 0.3 g | Carbs 43 g | Protein 0 g | Sodium 0 mg

10.1.5 Carrot Citrus Marmalade

Serves: 4-pint jars | Preparation time: 10 mins | Cooking Time: 35 mins

Ingredients:

- Grated carrots - 2 c.
- Water - 2 c.
- Orange - 1
- Sugar - 2½ c.
- Lemon - 1

Procedure:

1. Shred orange and lemon in a saucepan. Add the remaining ingredients. Next, boil the mixture.
2. Set heat to low, then parboil for 30 minutes.
3. Ladle the marmalade into the clean and hot jars. Leave ½" headspace.
4. Secure your jars with lids, then set in a water bath and process for 5 minutes.
5. You can serve or store it for later after cooling.

Nutrition per serving: Calories 43 | Fat 0 g | Carbs 11.3 g | Protein 0.1 g

10.1.6 Pineapple Marmalade

Serves: 8-pint jars | Preparation time: 10 mins | Cooking Time: 65 mins

Ingredients:

- Shredded pineapple flesh - 3½ c.
- Sugar - 4½ c.
- Water - 4 c.

- Sliced lemon - ½

Procedure:

1. Cook the pineapple and lemon in water in a saucepan for 20 minutes. Next, let it sit overnight.
2. Cook the pineapple mixture for 20 minutes.
3. Pour in the sugar, then whisk to mix.
4. Simmer for 25 minutes.
5. Finally, pour the marmalade into sterilized jars.
6. Secure with lids.
7. You can serve or store it for later after cooling.

Nutrition per serving: Calories 202 | Fat 0 g | Carbs 53 g | Sugar 53 g | Protein 0.2 g

10.1.7 Cherry Marmalade

Serves: 4-pint jars | Preparation time: 20 mins | Cooking Time: 30 mins

Ingredients:

- Lime - 4 tbsps.
- Cherries - 4 c.
- Sugar - 3½ c.
- Peeled and chopped orange - 2/3 c.

Procedure:

1. Boil the cherries, oranges, sugar and lime in a pan.
2. Next, cook the ingredients for 20 minutes at a slow boil after reducing the heat, stirring often. Slowly stir the pot while it continues to boil.
3. For the next 30 minutes, the mixture should be boiled hard, with continuous stirring, until it reaches a gel-like consistency. Take out the flames.
4. Pour the marmalade into the sterilized jars while it is still hot. To get rid of the air bubble, just add additional marmalade to the mixture. Use lids to keep them safe

Nutrition per serving: Calories 56 | Fat 0 g | Carbs 13 g | Protein 1 g

10.1.8 Pear Marmalade

Serves: 12-pint jars | Preparation time: 10 mins | Cooking Time: 10 mins

Ingredients:

- Lemon juice - 2 tbsps.
- Peeled & quartered ripe pears - 4
- Grated orange zest - 1 tbsp.
- Crushed pineapple - 8 oz.
- Pectin - 1.75 oz.
- Orange juice - ½ c.
- Sugar - 5½ c.

Procedure:

1. Pulse the pear slices.
2. In a saucepan, combine pear puree and pectin with the orange zest, lemon juice, orange juice, and pineapple juice, and boil.
3. Add sugar and cook for 1 minute as you stir constantly.
4. Finally, cool it.
5. Fill a clean jar with the marmalade.
6. You can store or serve.

Nutrition per serving: Calories 393 | Fat 0.1 g | Carbs 104.1 g | Sugar 99.8 g | Protein 0.4 g

10.1.9 Lemon Marmalade

Serves: 6 half pint jars | Preparation time: 15 mins | Cooking Time: 10 mins

Ingredients:

- Grapefruit - 1
- Powdered fruit pectin package - 1¾ oz.
- Water - 4 c.
- Lemons - 3
- Sugar - 4 c.

Procedure:

1. Peel, then cut 1"-long strips from lemon and grapefruit peels.
2. Boil the water, grapefruit and lemon in a Dutch oven. Next, add pectin and sugar. Cover the pot, then cook for 7 minutes.
3. Finally, allow cooling before you serve.

Nutrition per serving: Calories 50 | Fat 0.2 g | Carbs 3 g | Protein 0.3 g | Sodium 1 mg

10.2 JAMS

10.2.1 Blushing Peach Jam

Serves: 4 half pint jars | Preparation time: 15 mins | Cooking Time: 25 mins

Ingredients:

- Liquid fruit pectin - 16 oz.
- Granulated white sugar - 7 c.
- Lemon juice - ¼ c.
- Almond extract - 2 drops
- Crushed red raspberries - 2 c.
- Peeled, pitted, and crushed peaches - 2 c.

Procedure:

1. Add 2 tbsps. lemon juice to the peaches, and 2 tbsps. to the raspberries. Combine with sugar in a saucepan. Mix, then hard boil for 1 minute.
2. Remove your mixture from the heat, then add pectin. Next, stir and skim before adding the almond extract.
3. Pour into the jar, leaving ¼" headspace.
4. Finally, process jars for 10 minutes in boiling water.

Nutrition per serving: Calories 89 | Fat 1 g | Carbs 23 g | Protein 1 g

10.2.2 Strawberry Honey Jam

Serves: 6-pint jars | Preparation time: 25 mins | Cooking Time: 50 mins

Ingredients:

- Lemon juice - 1½ tbsps.
- Unpeeled and grated apple - 1½
- Honey - 3¾ c.
- Hulled and sliced strawberries - 6 lb.

Procedure:

1. Add everything into a pot, then boil. Next, lower the heat, then simmer for 50 minutes. Scrape and stir.
2. Mash the fruit and skim to your liking.
3. Adjust taste and consistency to your liking.
4. Ladle jams into jars with ¼" headspace.

5. Finally, process the jars for 10 minutes.
6. You can serve or store it after cooling.

Nutrition per serving: Calories 814 | Fat 1 g | Carbs 216 g | Protein 4 g | Potassium 853 mg | Sodium 14 mg

10.2.3 Blueberry Jam

Serves: 4-pint jars | Preparation time: 20 mins | Cooking Time: 22 mins

Ingredients:

- Lemon juice - 2 tbsps.
- Sugar - 2¾ c.
- Lemon zest - 2 tsps.
- Balsamic vinegar - 2 tbsps.
- Blueberries - 3¾ lb.

Procedure:

1. Combine everything in a Dutch oven, then boil for 12 minutes.
2. Next, pour the mixture into a bowl with a sieve. Drain blueberries from the juice and set them aside.
3. Next, pour the juice back into the kettle, then boil until it reaches 221°F. Add blueberries, then cook for 2 minutes.
4. Pour into jars leaving ¼" headspace.
5. Finally, process jars for 10 minutes,
6. You can serve or store it after cooling.

Nutrition per serving: Calories 32 | Fat 0.1 g | Carbs 8.3 g | Sugar 7.5 g | Protein 0.1 g | Potassium 13.8 mg

10.2.4 Mixed Berry Jam

Serves: 6 half pint jars | Preparation time: 15 mins | Cooking Time: 35 mins

Ingredients:

- Sugar - 3 c.
- Fruit pectin - 4½ tbsps.
- Crushed berries of your choice - 4 c.

Procedure:

1. In a saucepan, combine berries and gradually stir in pectin.
2. Next, boil the mixture as you stir it constantly.
3. Add sugar, stir, then boil, stirring constantly. Skim as needed.
4. Ladle jam into jars, leaving ¼" headspace.
5. Finally, process jars for 10 minutes.
6. You can serve or store it after cooling.

Nutrition per serving: Fat 1 g | Carbs 8 g | Sugar 7 g | Protein 1 g | Potassium 5 mg | Sodium 2 mg | Fiber 1

10.2.5 Plum Jam

Serves: 4 half pint jars | Preparation time: 22 mins | Cooking Time: 25 mins

Ingredients:

- Lemon juice - ½ c.
- Water - ½ c.
- Sugar - 3 c.
- Halved, pitted, and quartered plums - 3 lb.

Procedure:

1. In a saucepan, combine everything and boil for 20 minutes, stirring continuously.
2. Next, ladle jam into jars, leaving ¼" headspace.
3. Process jars for 10 minutes.
4. You can serve or store it after cooling.

Nutrition per serving: Calories 49 | Fat 0 g | Carbs 13 g | Sugar 12 g | Protein 0 g | Sodium 1 mg | Fiber 0 g

10.2.6 Strawberry Chia Jam

Serves: 8-pint jars | Preparation time: 10 mins | Cooking Time: 35 mins

Ingredients:

- Hulled strawberries - 2 lb.
- Fresh lemon juice - 1½ tbsps.
- Chia seeds - 2 tbsps.
- Maple syrup - ¼ c.

Procedure:

1. Add strawberries and maple syrup into the saucepan, then cook for 5 minutes.
2. Next, mash the strawberries.

3. Add lemon juice and chia seeds, then stir. Lower the heat, then cook for 30 minutes.
4. Next, let it cool.
5. You can serve or store it in a refrigerator.

Nutrition per serving: Calories 71 | Fat 1 g | Carbs 15.8 g | Sugar 11.5 g | Protein 1.2 g | Cholesterol 0 mg

10.2.7 Blueberry Chia Jam

Serves: 8-pint jars | Preparation time: 10 mins | Cooking Time: 18 mins

Ingredients:

- Blueberries - 3 c.
- Maple syrup - 3 tbsps.
- Chia seeds - 3 tbsps.

Procedure:

1. Add blueberries and maple syrup into the saucepan, then boil.
2. Next, cover and cook for 5 minutes.
3. Crush the berries.
4. Stir in chia seeds and reduce the heat. Stir it frequently, then cook for 13 minutes.
5. Next, let it cool.
6. Pour jam into a clean jar.
7. You can serve or store.

Nutrition per serving: Calories 64 | Fat 1.1 g | Carbs 13.5 g | Sugar 9.9 g | Protein 1 g | Cholesterol 0 mg

10.2.8 Blackberry Jam with Lemon Juice jam

Serves: 10-pint jars | Preparation time: 15 mins | Cooking Time: 26 mins

Ingredients:

- Sugar - 2 c.
- Blackberries - 5 c.
- Lemon juice - 2 tbsps.

Procedure:

1. Sterilize the bottles in a water bath canner.
2. Place all ingredients in a saucepan. Boil as you stir for 10 minutes. Simmer for 10 minutes after reducing the heat.
3. Next, allow it to cool.

4. Transfer the mixture to sterilized bottles. Close the lid.
5. Finally, set in a water bath canner, then process for 10 minutes.
6. You can serve or store it after cooling.

Nutrition per serving: Calories 196 | Fat 0.2 g | Carbs 49.7 g | Protein 1.7 g

10.2.9 Blackberry Jam

Serves: 4 half pint jars | Preparation time: 5 mins | Cooking Time: 15 mins

Ingredients:

- Crushed blackberries - 4 c.
- Sugar - 4 c.
- Water - 6 c.

Procedure:

1. Add the berries to a saucepan of boiling water after crushing them. Next, cook the mixture for 15 minutes. Add the sugar. Allow the sugar to dissolve for 1 hour before using.
2. Next, bring the mixture to a boil as you stir it constantly.
3. Fill sterilized jars halfway with the mixture, then screw with the lids.
4. Finally, set your jars in a water bath canner, then process for 5 minutes.

Nutrition per serving: Calories 83.3 | Fat 0.48 g | Carbs 21.87 g | Protein 4.47 g

10.3 PRESERVES

10.3.1 Blueberry Preserves

Serves: 6 | Preparation time: 10 mins | Cooking Time: 28 mins

Ingredients:

- Blueberries - 6 c.
- Lemon juice - 2
- Pectin - 3 tbsps.
- Sugar - 2 c.

Procedure:

1. Add blueberries and lemon juice into the pot, then boil as you stir frequently.
2. Mix ½ c. sugar and pectin and add it to the blueberries. Mix well, then return to boil.
3. Add remaining sugar and cook for 8 minutes.
4. Next, ladle blueberries into the clean jars, and leave ½" headspace.
5. Seal jars with lids, then process for 15 minutes in a boiling water bath.
6. You can serve or store it after cooling.

Nutrition per serving: Calories 339 | Fat 0.5 g | Carbs 88.7 g | Sugar 81.1 g | Protein 1.1 g | Cholesterol 0 mg

10.3.2 Preserved Lemons

Serves: 2 | Preparation time: 10 mins | Cooking Time: 15 mins

Ingredients:

- Rinsed lemons, score peel down length of lemons - 2
- Cinnamon stick - 1
- Bay leaf - 1
- Black peppercorns - 2 tsps.
- Whole cloves - 3
- Water - 3 c.
- Coriander seeds - 2 tsps.
- Kosher salt - 2 tbsps.

Procedure:

1. Boil the lemons, water, and salt in a saucepan. Simmer for 10 minutes after reducing the heat.
2. Transfer lemon to the clean canning jar. Next, reserve salt water.
3. Add bay leaf, cloves, cinnamon stick, coriander seeds, and black peppercorns into the lemon jar.
4. Pour the salt water over the lemons, then fill the jar.
5. Seal the jar with a lid.
6. Finally, you can serve or store it after cooling.

Nutrition per serving: Calories 22 | Fat 0.2 g | Carbs 6.8 g | Sugar 1.5 g | Protein 0.9 g | Cholesterol 0 mg

10.3.3 Preserved Fig

Serves: 14 | Preparation time: 10 mins | Cooking Time: 45 mins

Ingredients:

- Trimmed & roughly cut figs - 6 c.
- Lime zest - 1 tsp.
- Liquid pectin packet - 1
- Butter - 1 tsp.
- Water - ½ c.
- Lime juice - ¼ c.
- Sugar - 7 c.

Procedure:

1. Add the ingredients except for liquid pectin into a pot, then let sit for 30 minutes.
2. Next, boil the mixture for 10 minutes.
3. Stir in liquid pectin for 1 minute.
4. Next, let it cool.
5. Ladle fig into the clean jars, leave ½" headspace.
6. Seal jars with lids, then process for 20 minutes in a boiling water bath.
7. You can serve or store it after cooling.

Nutrition per serving: Calories 591 | Fat 1.1 g | Carbs 154.6 g | Sugar 140.9 g | Protein 2.8 g | Cholesterol 0 mg

10.3.4 Preserved Peach

Serves: 16 | Preparation time: 10 mins | Cooking Time: 30 mins

Ingredients:

- Peaches - 12
- Pectin - 2 oz.
- Sugar - 4½ c.

Procedure:

1. Crush 1 c. peaches in a saucepan. Next, add the remaining peaches into the saucepan. Boil, then cook for 20 minutes.
2. Boil after adding sugar. Slowly add pectin as you constantly stir for 1 minute.
3. Ladle peaches into the clean jars, and leave ½" headspace.
4. Seal jars with lids, then set them in a water bather canner and process for 10 minutes.
5. You can serve or store it after cooling.

Nutrition per serving: Calories 257 | Fat 0.3 g | Carbs 67 g | Sugar 66.8 g | Protein 1.1 g | Cholesterol 0 mg

10.3.5 Strawberry Preserves

Serves: 10 | Preparation time: 10 mins | Cooking Time: 20 mins

Ingredients:

- Strawberries - 2 lb.
- Vinegar - 2 tbsps.
- Sugar - 5 c.
- Salt – ¼ tsp.

Procedure:

1. Add the ingredients into a stockpot, then boil. Stir frequently, then cook for 20 minutes.
2. Next, ladle strawberry preserves into the clean jars, and leave ½" headspace.
3. Seal jars with lids, then process for 10 minutes in a boiling water bath.
4. You can serve or store it after cooling.

Nutrition per serving: Calories 405 | Fat 0.3 g | Carbs 107 g | Sugar 104.5 g | Protein 0.6 g | Cholesterol 0 mg

10.3.6 Vanilla Plum Preserves

Serves: 5 half pint jars | Preparation time: 25 mins | Cooking Time: 65 mins

Ingredients:

- Water - 1 c.
- Chopped, pitted red or black plums - 5 c.
- Granulated sugar - 4 c.
- Vanilla bean - 1

Procedure:

1. In a bowl, mix the sugar and plums. Cover, then let it sit for 18 hours in your refrigerator.
2. Boil the mixture in a pot after adding the water.
3. Scrape your vanilla bean before adding the paste to the pan.
4. Ensure that you stir the mixture frequently.
5. Boil for 40 minutes.
6. Next, ladle into 5 clean half-pint jars, leaving ¼" headspace. Top with 2-piece lids and rings and close until finger-tight.
7. Set in a water bath canner and process for about 15 minutes.
8. You can serve or store it after cooling.

Nutrition per serving: Calories 50 | Fat 0 g | Carbs 13 g | Protein 0 g

10.3.7 Peach Honey Preserves

Serves: 3 half pint jars | Preparation time: 20 mins | Cooking Time: 45 mins

Ingredients:

- Granulated sugar - 1½ c.
- Peeled & sliced peaches - 4 c.
- Honey - 1½ c.

Procedure:

1. In your bowl, combine the peaches, sugar, and honey. Cover, then let it sit for 18 hours in your refrigerator.
2. Transfer the mixture to a pot and boil as you stir frequently.
3. Boil gently for 40 minutes.
4. Ladle into 3 clean half-pint jars, leaving ¼" headspace. Top with 2-piece lids and rings and close until finger-tight.

5. Process for 15 minutes in a water bath canner.
6. You can serve or store it after cooling.

Nutrition per serving: Calories 56 | Fat 0 g | Carbs 14 g | Protein 0 g

10.3.8 Pineapple Lime Preserves

Serves: 3 half pint jars | Preparation time: 20 mins | Cooking Time: 30 mins

Ingredients:

- Chopped fresh pineapple - 4 c.
- Granulated sugar - 2½ c.
- Thinly sliced lime, seeds, and stem ends discarded - 1
- Water - 1 c.

Procedure:

1. In your pot, combine the pineapple, sugar, lime, and water and boil as you stir frequently.
2. Next, boil gently for 40 minutes.
3. Ladle into 3 clean half-pint jars, leaving ¼" headspace. Top with 2-piece lids and rings and close until finger-tight.
4. Finally, set your jars in a water bath canner, then process for 15 minutes.
5. You can serve or store it after cooling.

Nutrition per serving: Calories 50 | Fat 0 g | Carbs 13 g | Protein 0 g

10.3.9 Pear preserves

Serves: 3-pint jars | Preparation time: 40 mins | Cooking Time: 40 mins

Ingredients:

- Sugar - 3 c.
- Cored and quartered ripe pears - 6
- Thinly sliced and juiced lemon - 1
- Water - 2½ c.

Procedure:

1. Cook ½ c. sugar and ½ c. water for 2 minutes as you stir constantly.
2. Next, add pears, and cook for 15 minutes.
3. Add the remaining sugar and lemon juice. Stir, then cook for 25 minutes.
4. Cover, then put in the fridge for 24 minutes.

5. Put back to the heat, then boil.
6. Next, sterilize the jars and place the contents inside.
7. Close the jars.
8. In a pressure canner, process the jars for 5 minutes.
9. You can serve or store it after cooling.

Nutrition per serving: Calories 50 | Fat 0 g | Carbs 12 g | Sugar 10 g | Protein 0 g

10.4 SALSAS

10.4.1 Corn Salsa

Serves: 6 | Preparation time: 10 mins | Cooking Time: 25 mins

Ingredients:

- Cooked corn - 6 c.
- Vinegar - ½ c.
- Sugar - 1 c.
- Ground cumin - 2 tsps.
- Chopped fresh cilantro - 2 tbsps.
- Minced garlic cloves - 2
- Diced onion - 1 c.
- Diced poblano pepper - ¼ c.
- Diced jalapeno pepper - 2 tsps.
- Peeled, seeded, & chopped tomatoes - 2 lb.
- Salt - 2 tsps.

Procedure:

1. Add the ingredients into the saucepan and boil for 15 minutes.
2. Next, ladle salsa into the clean and hot jars.
3. Seal jars with lids, then process for 25 minutes in a boiling water bath.
4. Serve or store after cooling.

Nutrition per serving: Calories 295 | Fat 2 g | Carbs 70 g | Sugar 45 g | Protein 6 g | Cholesterol 0 mg

10.4.2 Tomato Salsa

Serves: 12 | Preparation time: 10 mins | Cooking Time: 25 mins

Ingredients:

- Peel, cored, and chopped tomatoes - 10 c.
- Chopped cilantro - 2 tbsps.
- Chopped garlic cloves - 3
- Apple cider vinegar - 1¼ c.
- Chopped chili peppers - 2½ c.
- Chopped onions - 5 c.
- Chopped green bell peppers - 5 c.
- Kosher salt - 1 tbsp.

Procedure:

1. Add the ingredients into a stockpot and boil. Next, reduce heat and simmer for 10 minutes.
2. Ladle salsa into the clean and hot jars.
3. Seal jars with lids, then process for 15 minutes in a boiling water bath.
4. Serve or store after cooling.

Nutrition per serving: Calories 93 | Fat 0.9 g | Carbs 20 g | Sugar 11.8 g | Protein 3.2 g | Cholesterol 0 mg

10.4.3 Peach Tomato Salsa

Serves: 16 | Preparation time: 10 mins | Cooking Time: 10 mins

Ingredients:

- Peeled & chopped peaches - 2
- Pepper - 1/8 tsp.
- Brown sugar - 2 tsps.
- Lime juice - ½ tsp.
- Vinegar - 2 tsps.
- Chopped green chilies - 4 oz.
- Minced garlic clove - 1
- Dried cilantro - ½ tbsp.
- Chopped onion - ¼
- Chopped tomato - 1
- Salt - ¼ tsp.

Procedure:

1. Add the ingredients into a bowl and mix.
2. Ladle salsa in a clean jar.
3. Serve or store.

Nutrition per serving: Calories 34 | Fat 0.5 g | Carbs 7.5 g | Sugar 5.2 g | Protein 1 g | Cholesterol 0 mg

10.4.4 Peach Salsa

Serves: 8 | Preparation time: 10 mins | Cooking Time: 20 mins

Ingredients:

- Peeled, pitted & diced peaches - 8 c.
- Diced onion - 2 c.

- Lime juice - 1 c.
- Diced chili peppers - 2 c.
- Diced tomatoes - 4 c.
- Vinegar - 1½ c.
- Minced garlic cloves - 6
- Sea salt - 1 tbsp.

Procedure:

1. Add the ingredients into a saucepan, then boil.
2. Simmer for 10 minutes as you stir frequently after reducing the heat.
3. Ladle salsa into the clean jars.
4. Seal jar with lids.
5. Finally, set in a water bath canner, then process for about 15 minutes.
6. You can serve or store after cooling.

Nutrition per serving: Calories 116 | Fat 1 g | Carbs 25 g | Sugar 20 g | Protein 3 g

10.4.5 Zesty Salsa

Serves: 6-pint jars | Preparation time: 20 mins | Cooking Time: 20 mins

Ingredients:

- Chopped and seeded green bell peppers - 5 c.
- Hot pepper sauce - 1 tsp.
- Chopped onions - 5 c.
- Salt - 1 tbsp.
- Chopped cilantro - 2 tbsps.
- Finely chopped garlic cloves - 3
- Cider vinegar - 1¼ c.
- Chopped and seeded chili peppers - 2½ c.
- Chopped, cored, and peeled tomatoes - 10 c.

Procedure:

1. Combine everything in a saucepan.
2. Boil as you stir constantly. Reduce heat, then simmer as you stir for 10 minutes.
3. Ladle hot salsa into hot jars with ½" headspace.
4. Process for 15 minutes,
5. Serve or store after cooling.

Nutrition per serving: Calories 15 | Fat 0 g | Carbs 3 g | Sugar 2 g | Sodium 76 mg

10.4.6 Spicy Corn Salsa

Serves: 4-pint jars | Preparation time: 25 mins | Cooking Time: 30 mins

Ingredients:

- Chipotle chile powder - ½ tsp.
- Ground cumin - 2 tsps.
- Kosher salt - 4 tsps.
- Diced white onions - 1 c.
- Minced fresh garlic - 2 tbsps.
- Sugar - ¼ c.
- Distilled white vinegar - 1 c.
- Chopped fresh cilantro - ¼ c.
- Finely diced jalapeños - 2
- Peeled, seeded, cored, and diced tomatoes - 3 c.
- Diced poblanos - 1 c.
- Corn kernels - 3 c.

Procedure:

1. Combine the ingredients in a pot. Boil, then simmer for 15 minutes after reducing the heat.
2. Ladle salsa into jars, leaving ½" headspace
3. Finally, process jars for 15 minutes.
4. Serve or store after cooling.

Nutrition per serving: Calories 25 | Fat 0 g | Carbs 6 g | Sodium 244 mg | Protein 1 g

10.4.7 Mango Pineapple Salsa

Serves: 4-pint jars | Preparation time: 27 mins | Cooking Time: 30 mins

Ingredients:

- Minced garlic cloves - 2
- Grated fresh ginger - 1 tsp.
- Cider vinegar - ¼ c.
- Lime juice - ¼
- Sugar - 1/3 c.
- Salt - ½ tsp.
- Finely chopped jalapeños - ¼ c.
- Red sweet pepper - 1 c.
- Sweet onion - 1 c.
- Peeled and chopped mangoes - 2 c.
- Pineapple - 3 c.

- Cored and chopped ripe tomatoes - 4 c.

Procedure:

1. Combine the ingredients in a pot. Then, boil to a simmer for 10 minutes as you stir occasionally.
2. Next, ladle salsa into jars with ½" headspace.
3. Finally, process jars for 20 minutes in boiling water.
4. Serve or store after cooling.

Nutrition per serving: Calories 17 | Fat 0 g | Carbs 4 g | Protein 0 g

10.4.8 Corn and Cherry Tomato Salsa

Serves: 6-pint jars | Preparation time: 26 mins | Cooking Time: 28 mins

Ingredients:

- Seeded and minced jalapeño peppers - 2
- Lime juice - ½ c and salt - 2 tsps.
- Finely chopped red onion - 1 c.
- Corn kernels - 2 c.
- Chopped fresh cilantro - ½ c.
- Roughly chopped cherry tomatoes - 5 lb.

Procedure:

1. Add the ingredients into a pot. Boil, then simmer for 10 minutes after reducing the heat as you stir occasionally.
2. Ladle salsa into jars, leaving ½" headspace.
3. Finally, process jars for 15 minutes in boiling water.
4. Serve or store after cooling.

Nutrition per serving: Calories 48 | Fat 0.8 g | Carbs 10.2 g | Protein 1.1 g | Sodium 0.2 mg

10.4.9 Mexican-Inspired Salsa

Serves: 8-pint jars | Preparation time: 50 mins | Cooking Time: 30 mins

Ingredients:

- Chopped garlic cloves - 8
- White vinegar - 1 c.
- Chopped jalapeños - 4
- Diced onion - 2½ c.
- Chopped tomatoes - 9 c.

- Diced green bell peppers - 2½ c.
- Tomato paste - 1½ c.
- Canning salt - 6 tsps.

Procedure:

1. Boil the tomatoes for 1 minute in water. Next, set your tomatoes aside to cool.
2. Peel the tomatoes' skin, then add to a pot with the other ingredients.
3. Simmer for 30 minutes.
4. Next, transfer the salsa to sterile jars, then seal.
5. Finally, set your jars in water bath canner, then process for 30 minutes.
6. Serve or store after cooling.

Nutrition per serving: Calories 23 | Fat 0.3 g | Carbs 5.2 g | Protein 1.1 g

10.4.10   Red Onion & Tomato Salsa

Serves: 8-pint jars | Preparation time: 45 mins | Cooking Time: 20 mins

Ingredients:

- Quartered tomatoes - 10 lb.
- Tomato paste - 3 c.
- White vinegar - 1¾ c.
- Hot pepper sauce - ½ tsp.
- Canning salt - ¼ c.
- Seeded and chopped jalapeno peppers - 5
- Chopped green peppers - 4
- Minced garlic cloves - 15
- Chopped celery rib - 1
- Chopped red onions - 3
- Chopped sweet red pepper - 1
- Sugar - ½ c.

Procedure:

1. In a pot, boil your tomatoes for 20 minutes. Next, reserve the cooking liquid after draining.
2. Return to your pot and add the remaining ingredients. Cook for 1 hour.
3. Next, transfer to sterile jars, then seal.
4. Finally, set your jars in a water bath canner, then process for 30 minutes.
5. Serve or store after cooling.

Nutrition per serving: Calories 14 | Fat 0 g | Carbs 3 g | Protein 0 g

10.5 SAUCES

10.5.1 Blueberry Sauce

Serves: 6 | Preparation time: 10 mins | Cooking Time: 20 mins

Ingredients:

- Blueberries - 2 lb.
- Sugar - 1 lb.
- Lemon juice - 1
- Cornstarch - 1½ tbsps.

Procedure:

1. Add blueberries and sugar to a bowl, then mash berries. Next, cover and let it sit overnight.
2. Take 2 tbsp. blueberry juice. In a bowl, whisk the blueberry juice, lemon juice and cornstarch, then set aside.
3. Add the blueberry and sugar mixture into the pan and boil. Next, add the cornstarch mixture, then cook for 10 minutes as you stir constantly.
4. Finally, ladle sauce into the clean jar.
5. You can serve or store.

Nutrition per serving: Calories 378 | Fat 0.5 g | Carbs 99 g | Sugar 90 g | Protein 1.2 g | Cholesterol 0 mg

10.5.2 Pear Sauce

Serves: 8 | Preparation time: 10 mins | Cooking Time: 30 mins

Ingredients:

- Ground cinnamon - 1 tsp
- Peeled, cored, and chopped pears - 8
- Vanilla extract - ½ tsp.
- Lemon juice - 2 tsps.
- Ground ginger - ½ tsp
- Water - ¼ c.

Procedure:

1. Add the ingredients into a saucepan. Boil, then simmer for 30 minutes after reducing the heat.
2. Next, puree the sauce using a blender.

3. Pour sauce into a clean jar.
4. You can serve or store.

Nutrition per serving: Calories 123 | Fat 0.3 g | Carbs 32 g | Sugar 20 g | Protein 0.9 g

10.5.3 Strawberry Sauce

Serves: 14 | Preparation time: 10 mins | Cooking Time: 20 mins

Ingredients:

- Sliced strawberries - 2 lb.
- Sugar - 1 c.
- Water - 2 tsps.
- Pectin - ½ tsp.

Procedure:

1. Add strawberries into a pot, then mash.
2. Next, reserve 4 tbsps. of strawberry juice.
3. In a bowl, whisk 4 tbsps. of strawberry juice and pectin, then set aside.
4. Boil after adding sugar and water to the strawberries.
5. Next, gradually add the pectin mixture as you stir for 2 minutes.
6. Finally, ladle sauce into the clean jar. Leave ½" headspace.
7. Seal jars with lids, then process for 10 minutes in a boiling water bath.
8. Serve or store after cooling.

Nutrition per serving: Calories 75 | Fat 0.2 g | Carbs 19.3 g | Sugar 17.5 g | Protein 0.4 g

10.5.4 Apple Sauce

Serves: 6 | Preparation time: 10 mins | Cooking Time: 1 hr. 40 mins

Ingredients:

- Hot peppers - 3 lb.
- Peel, cored, and chopped apples - 2
- Chopped onions - 2
- Turmeric - ½ tsp.

- Mustard seeds - 1/3 c.
- Minced garlic - 3 tbsps.
- Vinegar - 2 c.
- Salt - 2 tbsps.

Procedure:

1. Add the ingredients into a saucepan, then boil.
2. Reduce heat, then simmer for 60 minutes.
3. Next, puree the sauce using a blender.
4. Ladle sauce into the clean jars. Leave ½" headspace.
5. Seal jar with lids.
6. Finally, set in a water bath, then process for 15 minutes.
7. You can serve or store after cooling.

Nutrition per serving: Calories 180 | Fat 3 g | Carbs 32.7 g | Sugar 20 g | Protein 6 g

10.5.5 Roasted Garlic Sauce

Serves: 6-pint jars | Preparation time: 30 mins | Cooking Time: 60 mins

Ingredients:

- Roasted and chopped garlic cloves - 6
- Lemon juice - 6 tbsps.
- Olive oil - 3 tbsps.
- Ground black pepper - 1 tsp.
- Halved, seeded, and roasted green sweet peppers - 4
- Kosher salt - 2 tbsps.
- Packed brown sugar - 3 tbsps.
- Peeled ripe tomatoes - 12 lb.
- Balsamic vinegar - 1 tbsp.
- Snipped fresh basil leaves - 2 c.
- Snipped fresh herbs (oregano, thyme, parsley) - 1 c.

Procedure:

1. In a pot, mix the garlic, olive oil, tomatoes, brown sugar, salt, vinegar, and pepper. Boil the mixture for 52 minutes.
2. Next, add the green peppers, then continue boiling for 10 minutes.
3. Pull it from heat, then stir in the basil and herbs.
4. Next, spoon 1 tbsp. of the lemon juice into each of your sterile jars.

5. Pour the sauce into jars with the lemon juice, leaving a ½" headspace.
6. Set your jars in a water bath, then process for 35 minutes.
7. Serve or store after cooling.

Nutrition per serving: Calories 377 | Fat 24.09 g | Carbs 16 g | Protein 25.6 g

10.5.6 Lemon Strawberry Sauce

Serves: 2-pint jars | Preparation time: 15 mins | Cooking Time: 15 mins

Ingredients:

- Lemon juice - ¼ c.
- Strawberries - 2 lb.
- Granulated sugar - 4 c.

Procedure:

1. In a bowl, crush the strawberries.
2. Next, mix the strawberries, lemon juice, and sugar in a pot.
3. Stir as you simmer, then increase the heat and boil for 15 minutes. Ensure you stir as it cooks.
4. Next, spoon the sauce into a jar, then transfer the sauce, leaving ½" headspace.
5. Set in a water bath, then process for 10 minutes.
6. You can serve or store after cooling.

Nutrition per serving: Calories 64 | Fat 2.8 g | Carbs 10.2 g | Protein 0.9 g

10.5.7 Summer Tomato Sauce

Serves: 8 half pint jars | Preparation time: 5 mins | Cooking Time: 0 mins

Ingredients:

- Extra-virgin olive oil - 2 tbsps.
- Minced garlic cloves - 3
- Chopped red onion - 1
- Halved tomatoes - 3 lb.
- Red pepper flakes – ¼ tsp.
- Chopped thyme - ½ tsp.
- Chopped oregano - 1 tsp.
- Chopped basil - 1 tsp.
- Chopped parsley - 1 tbsp.

- Sea salt - ¼ tsp.
- Black Pepper - ¼ tsp.

Procedure:

1. Warm your nonstick skillet, then add oil. Next, sauté onion and garlic for 3 minutes.
2. Stir in tomatoes, red pepper flakes, thyme, oregano, basil, parsley, salt, and black pepper. Simmer for 30 minutes after lowering the heat.
3. Next, purée the sauce in a food processor.
4. Fill your sterilized jars halfway with the mixture and seal.
5. Finally, set your jars in a water bath canner, then process for 5 minutes.
6. Serve or store after cooling.

Nutrition per serving: Calories 53 | Fat 0.3 g | Carbs 12.9 g | Protein 0.4 g

10.5.8 Pizza Sauce

Serves: 4-pint jars | Preparation time: 40 mins | Cooking Time: 50 mins

Ingredients:

- Chopped parsley - 2 tbsps.
- Ripe tomatoes - 28
- Celery seed - 1 tsp.
- Minced yellow onions - 2
- Olive oil - 3 tbsps.
- Black pepper - 1 tsp.
- Oregano - 1 tbsp.
- Dry basil - 1 tbsp.
- Lemon juice - 2 tbsps.
- Dry rosemary - 1 tsp.
- Minced garlic cloves - 4
- Kosher salt - 2 tsps.
- White sugar - 1 tbsp.

Procedure:

1. Peel the tomatoes, then blanch for 3 minutes in boiling water.
2. Next, cook the onions and garlic for 4 minutes in a saucepan with olive oil.

3. Add the tomato puree and the remaining ingredients.Boil, then simmer for 45 minutes after reducing the heat.
4. Distribute the sauce into jars.
5. Set your jars in a water bath canner, then process for 25 minutes.
6. Serve or store after cooling.

Nutrition per serving: Calories 85 | Fat 3.1 g | Carbs 7.2 g | Protein 1.2 g

10.5.9 Cranberry Sauce

Serves: 12 | Preparation time: 30 mins | Cooking Time: 25 mins

Ingredients:

- Water - 1 c.
- Washed cranberries - 10 c.
- Port wine - 2 c.
- Sugar - 4 c.
- Red vinegar - 4 tbsps.
- Cinnamon sticks - 8
- Canning jars and lids

Procedure:

1. Begin by heating a saucepan, then combining the vinegar, sugar, and water.
2. Increase the heat as you stir. Next, add the cranberries and wine when the mixture begins boiling.
3. Boil for 5 minutes. Next, reduce the heat. Stir, then pull it off heat.
4. Ladle ½" of the mix, then turn into each jar, ensuring you include 2 cinnamon sticks in each one after cooling.
5. Process for 15 minutes in a water bath.
6. Serve or store after cooling.

Nutrition per serving: Calories 418.3 | Carbs 107.8 g | Protein 0.6 g | Fiber 2.8 mg

10.6 PICKLES

10.6.1 Pickled Cucumbers

Serves: 6 | Preparation time: 10 mins | Cooking Time: 60 mins

Ingredients:

- Water - ½ c.
- Apple cider vinegar - ½ c.
- Sugar - 1 tbsp.
- Thinly sliced cucumber - 1
- Kosher salt - 1½ tsps.

Procedure:

1. In a bowl, mix the sugar, water, vinegar, and salt. Next, stir.
2. Add sliced cucumbers into the bowl and let soak for 1 hour.
3. Pour pickled cucumbers into the clean jar and seal the jar with a lid.
4. Once a jar is open, then store it in the refrigerator.

Nutrition per serving: Calories 19 | Fat 0.1 g | Carbs 4 g | Sugar 2.9 g | Protein 0.3 g

10.6.2 Pickled Jalapeno

Serves: 2 | Preparation time: 10 mins | Cooking Time: 15 mins

Ingredients:

- Jalapeno peppers sliced into rings - 10
- Oregano - ½ tsp.
- Crushed garlic clove - 1
- White sugar - 3 tbsps.
- Vinegar - ¾ c.
- Water - ¾ c.
- Kosher salt - 1 tbsp.

Procedure:

1. Add water, oregano, garlic, sugar, vinegar, and salt into a saucepan and boil over heat.
2. Stir in jalapeno peppers.
3. Next, allow the mixture to cool.

4. Pour pickled jalapeno with brine into a clean jar.
5. You can serve or store.

Nutrition per serving: Calories 119 | Fat 0.9 g | Carbs 24.8 g | Sugar 20.8 g | Protein 1.2 g

10.6.3 Pickled Carrots

Serves: 8 | Preparation time: 10 mins | Cooking Time: 30 mins

Ingredients:

- Peeled carrots sliced into sticks - 1 lb.
- Apple cider vinegar - 2/3 c.
- Sugar - 1 tbsp.
- Water - 1/3 c.
- Sea salt - ½ tsp.

Procedure:

1. Pack the carrot into a clean jar.
2. Add water, vinegar, sugar, and salt into a saucepan, then cook for 20 minutes.
3. Pour hot brine over carrots in a jar.
4. You can serve or store.

Nutrition per serving: Calories 33 | Fat 0 g | Carbs 7.3 g | Sugar 4.4 g | Protein 0.5 g

10.6.4 Pickled Banana Peppers

Serves: 4 | Preparation time: 10 mins | Cooking Time: 10 mins

Ingredients:

- Seeded banana peppers sliced into the rings - 1 lb.
- Sugar - 1 1/3 c.
- Vinegar - 4 c.
- Celery seeds - 1 tsp.
- Mustard seeds - 1 tsp.

Procedure:

1. Add vinegar, celery, mustard, and sugar to a saucepan and boil.
2. Next, add the banana peppers into the clean jars, then pour hot brine over the peppers.

3. Seal the jar with a lid.
4. You can serve or store.

Nutrition per serving: Calories 315 | Fat 0.4 g | Carbs 70 g | Sugar 70 g | Protein 0.6 g

10.6.5 Pickled Cherry Tomatoes

Serves: 4 | Preparation time: 10 mins | Cooking Time: 10 mins

Ingredients:

- Water - 2 c.
- Vinegar - 1 c.
- Cherry tomatoes - 4 c.
- Fresh rosemary sprigs - 2
- Garlic cloves - 2
- Salt - ½ tsp.

Procedure:

1. Boil vinegar, water, and salt in a saucepan. Next, simmer for 10 minutes after reducing the heat.
2. Pack cherry tomatoes in clean jars.
3. Next, add garlic cloves and rosemary over the tomatoes.
4. Pour hot vinegar solution over tomatoes. Leave ¼" headspace.
5. Seal jar with lids.
6. Finally, set your jars in a water bath canner, then process for 10 minutes.
7. You can serve or store it after cooling.

Nutrition per serving: Calories 45 | Fat 0.5 g | Carbs 8 g | Sugar 5 g | Protein 2 g

10.6.6 Pickled Asparagus

Serves: 4 | Preparation time: 10 mins | Cooking Time: 10 mins

Ingredients:

- Fresh asparagus spears, trim ends - 1 lb.
- Sugar - 1½ tsp.
- Fresh dill sprigs - 3
- Peeled garlic cloves - 2
- Vinegar - 1½ c.
- Black peppercorns - ½ tsp.
- Water - 1 c.
- Salt - 2 tbsps.

Procedure:

1. Pack asparagus spears into the jars.
2. Next, boil water, sugar, salt, dill sprigs, peppercorns, and vinegar in a saucepan as you stir.
3. Pour hot water mixture over asparagus. Leave ½" headspace.
4. Seal the jar with lids.
5. You can serve or store it after cooling.

Nutrition per serving: Calories 40 | Fat 0.2 g | Carbs 6 g | Sugar 3 g | Protein 2.2 g

10.6.7 Pickled Beets

Serves: 12 | Preparation time: 10 mins | Cooking Time: 40 mins

Ingredients:

- Clean beets - 24
- Cinnamon stick - 1
- Sugar - 2 c.
- Vinegar - 3½ c.
- Water – 8 c.
- Salt – ½ tsp.

Procedure:

1. Add beets into boiling water, then cook for 10 minutes.
2. Drain beets, then peel and cut into chunks.
3. Boil 1½ c. water, vinegar, cinnamon, sugar, and salt in a saucepan.
4. Next, simmer for 15 minutes after reducing the heat. Discard cinnamon stick.
5. Pack beets into the clean and hot jars. Leave ¼" headspace.
6. Pour hot water mixture over beets. Leave ¼" headspace.
7. Seal jar with lids.
8. Finally, set your jars in a water bath canner, then process for 30 minutes.
9. You can serve or store it after cooling.

Nutrition per serving: Calories 211 | Fat 0.5 g | Carbs 50 g | Sugar 44 g | Protein 2.5 g

10.6.8 Spicy Rosemary Pickled Carrots

Serves: 6-pint jars | Preparation time: 5 mins | Cooking Time: 15 mins

Ingredients:

- Vinegar - 3 c.
- Water - 3 c.
- White sugar - ¼ c.
- Pickling salt - ¼ c.
- Black peppercorns - 2 tbsps.
- Peeled garlic cloves - 6
- Red chili peppers - 6
- Peeled carrots sliced into 4" -long stocks at ½" wide - 4 lbs.
- Rosemary sprigs - 6

Procedure:

1. In a pot, combine peppercorns, sugar, water, salt, and vinegar. Next, boil, then simmer for 5 minutes after reducing the heat.
2. Add 1 chili pepper and 1 garlic clove into each jar, one at a time. Ensure you pack it tightly with carrot stocks, then add in the rosemary sprig halfway through.
3. Pour the vinegar solution over the carrots. Ensure you leave ¼" head space.
4. Finally, process for 15 minutes.
5. You can serve or store it after cooling.

Nutrition per serving: Calories 57 | Fat 1 g | Carbs 11 g | Protein 1 g

10.6.9 Dill Pickles

Serves: 9-pint jars | Preparation time: 25 mins | Cooking Time: 10 mins

Ingredients:

- Cucumbers - 6
- Water - 3 c.
- Pickling salt - ¼ c.
- White vinegar - 2 c.
- Fresh dill sprigs - 2
- Peeled garlic head and cloves separated - 1

Procedure:

1. Begin by slicing the cucumbers twice lengthwise, then set them aside.
2. In a pot, combine water, pickling salt, and vinegar. Next, boil for 10 minutes.

3. Place the cucumbers in hot jars, and add the brining solution (the vinegar solution) to the jars, leaving ½" space at the top.
4. Next, add dill and garlic cloves around the cucumbers.
5. Finally, process in a boiling water bath for 15 minutes.
6. Serve or store after cooling.

Nutrition per serving: Calories 81 | Fat 3.8 g | Carbs 13 g | Protein 3.1 g

10.6.10   Pickled Mushroom

Serves: 30 | Preparation time: 5 mins | Cooking Time: 15 mins

Ingredients:

- Sugar - ¼ c.
- Dried tarragon - ¼ tsp.
- Pepper - ½ tsp.
- Canola oil - 1½ c.
- White vinegar - 2 c.
- Halved and sliced onions - 2
- Canning salt - 2 tbsps.
- Minced garlic cloves - 3
- Mushrooms - 5 lb.

Procedure:

1. Ensure you sterilize your jars.
2. Add the ingredients to a clean pot and boil.
3. Simmer for 10 minutes before you serve.
4. Ladle the hot mixture into the jars, leaving a ½" headspace.
5. Process the jars for 20 minutes in a hot water canner.
6. You can serve or store it after cooling.

Nutrition per serving: Calories 18 | Fat 1 g | Carbs 2 g | Protein 1 g

10.6.11   Radish Pickle

Serves: 2-pint jars | Preparation time: 20 mins | Cooking Time: 15 mins

Ingredients:

- Whole cumin seeds - ½ tsp.
- Sugar - 1½ tbsps.
- Kosher salt - 1 tsp.

- Water - 1/3 c.
- White wine vinegar - 2/3 c.
- Thinly sliced radishes - 3 c.

Procedure:

1. Begin by rinsing the radishes in a strainer, then drain the water.
2. Next, boil water and vinegar in a pot. Add sugar, cumin seeds and salt and stir.
3. Let it cool before you serve.
4. Now, prepare the radishes in storage jars, ensuring you leave room for canning liquid. Leave a ¼" headspace while you pour the vinegar liquid over the radishes.
5. Finally, process the jars for 15 minutes in the hot water bath.
6. You can serve or store it after cooling.

Nutrition per serving: Calories 16.7 | Fat 0.1 g | Carbs 3.9 g | Protein 0.3 g | Sodium 591 mg

10.6.12   Mexican-Style Jalapeño and Carrot Pickles

Serves: 5-pint jars | Preparation time: 60 mins | Cooking Time: 20 mins

Ingredients:

- Olive oil - 1/3 c.
- Stemmed jalapeño peppers cut into ½" thick slices - 1 lb.
- Carrots cut into ½" thick slices - 4
- White or yellow onions, cut into ½" slices - 3
- Peeled garlic cloves - 8
- Distilled white vinegar - 4 c.
- Diamond Crystal kosher salt - 2 tbsps.
- Bay leaves - 2
- Mexican oregano - 1 tbsp.
- Black peppercorns - 1 tbsp.
- Sugar - 1 tbsp.
- Water – 3 c.

Procedure:

1. Add the oil to a saucepan. Next, cook the carrots, onions, garlic, jalapeno, and other seasonings in the saucepan as you stir for 10 minutes

2. Heat the vinegar, salt, bay leaves, oregano, peppercorns, and sugar in a saucepan. Next, pour in the water and simmer.
3. Allow for flavor infusion before you add the mixture to the veggies.
4. Cook for 10 minutes as you stir often.
5. Fill your jars with the mixture, allowing ½" headspace.
6. Finally, set your jars in a water bath canner, then process for 10 minutes.
7. You can serve or store it after cooling.

Nutrition per serving: Calories 74 | Fat 0.2 g | Carbs 15 g | Sodium 852 mg | Protein 2.1

10.6.13   Pickled Brussels sprouts

Serves: 6 | Preparation time: 20 mins | Cooking Time: 30 mins

Ingredients:

- Smashed garlic cloves - 12
- Black peppercorns - 15
- Water - 2 c.
- Halved Brussels sprouts with cut stem ends - 3 lbs.
- Vinegar - 5 c.
- Dill heads - 6
- Salt – ¼ tsp.
- Black pepper – ½ tsp.

Procedure:

1. Boil water, vinegar, and salt in a pot.
2. Next, add peppercorns and pepper to each dill and garlic jar.
3. Pack the Brussels sprouts into the jars as you allow a ½" headroom.
4. Cover Brussels sprouts with boiling water mixture, then stir. Allow for a ½" headroom. Next, put the lids on the jars.
5. Finally, set in a water vath canner, then process for about 10 minutes.
6. You can serve or store it after cooling.

Nutrition per serving: Calories 150 | Fat 0.9 g | Carbs 24.6 g | Sugar 5.7 g | Protein 8.1 g

10.6.14   Mustard Pickles

Serves: 16 | **Preparation time:** 8½ hrs. | **Cooking Time:** 10 mins

Ingredients:

- Dry mustard powder - 1 tbsp.
- Ground dried turmeric - 1 tbsp.
- Celery seed - ½ tsp.
- White sugar - 2 c.
- White vinegar - 2 c.
- Cold water - 8
- All-purpose flour - 2 tbsps.
- Pickling salt - 2 tbsps.
- Sliced onion - 4 c.
- Sliced cucumbers – 8
- Black pepper – ¼ tsp.

Procedure:

1. Mix the salt, pepper, onions, and cucumbers in a basin. Next, cover the cucumbers with water.
2. Let it sit for 10 hours.
3. Next, drain and rinse the onion and cucumbers.
4. Ensure you sterilize your 41-quart jars together with their lids.
5. In a saucepan, mix sugar and flour. Next, combine celery seed, mustard powder, turmeric, and vinegar. Fill the pot with water. Mix, then boil. Next, simmer for 10 minutes.
6. Fill hot jars to within ½" of the rim with the ingredients.
7. Finally, set your jars in a water bath canner, then process for 10 minutes.
8. Serve or store after cooling.

Nutrition per serving: Calories 138 | Fat 0.5 g | Carbs 33.9 g | Protein 1.5 g | Sodium 880 mg

10.6.15   Pickled Southern Peaches

Serves: 30 | **Preparation time:** 20 mins | **Cooking Time:** 26 mins

Ingredients:

- Cinnamon sticks - 5
- Blanched and peeled fresh clingstone peaches - 4 lb.
- Sugar - 4 c.
- Whole cloves - 2 tbsps.
- White vinegar - 1 c.

- Water - 1 c.

Procedure:

1. Fill a pot halfway with vinegar and water. Next, add sugar, then boil. After a rolling boil, cook for 5 minutes as you stir constantly.
2. Next, toss the peaches into the boiling liquid with a few cloves inserted into each one. Boil for 20 minutes.
3. Ensure you submerge the components in the vinegar solution, place the peaches in clean, sterilized jars, and seal.
4. Next, add a cinnamon stick into each jar, then seal.
5. Set your jars in a water bath canner, then process for 10 minutes.
6. You can serve or store it after cooling.

10.6.16   Vinegary Carrot with Dill Pickles

Serves: 24 | **Preparation time:** 10 mins | **Cooking Time:** 10 mins

Ingredients:

- Peeled and trimmed carrots - 6 lb.
- Crushed garlic cloves - 6
- Canning salt - 4 tbsps.
- Water - 4 c.
- Apple cider vinegar - 4 c.
- Dill seeds - 1 tbsp.
- Black peppercorns - ½ tbsp.
- Brown sugar - ½ c.

Procedure:

1. Prepare your carrots by cutting them into long spears. For the size of your carrot pieces, you'll need to take into consideration your jars.
2. Bring a pot of salt, sugar, vinegar, and water to a boil.
3. Pour the carrots into your jars, then distribute the remaining spices (cloves, dill seeds and peppercorns) equally among the jars.
4. Leave a ½-inch headspace when adding the brine to the jars' contents.
5. Process carrot pickles for 10 minutes, depending on altitude, by wiping the jar's rim and screwing on the lid.

Nutrition per serving: Calories 82 | Fat 0.1 g | Carbs 18 g | Protein 1.3 g | Sodium 1251 mg

10.7 CHUTNEY

10.7.1 Sweet & Sour Cherry Chutney

Serves: 8 | Preparation time: 10 mins | Cooking Time: 30 mins

Ingredients:

- Pitted & chopped fresh cherries - 1¼ lb.
- Olive oil - 1 tbsp.
- Brown sugar - 2 tbsps.
- Whole-grain mustard - 1 tbsp.
- Red wine vinegar - ½ c.
- Grated ginger - 1 tsp.
- Minced garlic clove - 1
- Dried currants - 1/3 c.
- Diced onion - ½
- Kosher salt - 1 tsp.

Procedure:

1. Heat oil in a pot.
2. Next, sauté the garlic and onions for 3 minutes.
3. Add vinegar, then continue cooking for about 3 minutes.
4. Next, add cherries, mustard, sugar, ginger, currants, and salt and stir. Next, simmer for 30 minutes as you stir frequently.
5. Pour chutney into a clean jar after cooling.
6. You can serve or store.

Nutrition per serving: Calories 115 | Fat 1.8 g | Carbs 23.7 g | Sugar 2.8 g | Protein 0.4 g

10.7.2 Peach Chutney

Serves: 4 | Preparation time: 10 mins | Cooking Time: 12 mins

Ingredients:

- Peeled and diced peaches - 1¼ c.
- Brown sugar - 1 tbsp.
- Ground cardamom - ¼ tsp.
- Cinnamon - ¼ tsp
- Vegetable oil - ½ tbsp.
- Diced garlic clove- 1
- Apple cider vinegar - 2 tbsps.
- Diced ginger - 1 tsp.
- Diced onion - ¼

Procedure:

1. Add oil to a saucepan over heat.
2. Next, saute the garlic, ginger, and onion for 3 minutes.
3. Add vinegar, sugar, cardamom, and cinnamon and stir.
4. Add peaches and mix as you cook for 10 minutes.
5. Pour chutney into a clean jar after cooling.
6. You can serve or store.

Nutrition per serving: Calories 50 | Fat 1.9 g | Carbs 8.1 g | Sugar 6.9 g | Protein 0.6 g

10.7.3 Apple Chutney

Serves: 15 | Preparation time: 10 mins | Cooking Time: 15 mins

Ingredients:

- Red chili powder - 1 tsp.
- Peeled & diced apples - 6
- Cinnamon stick - 1
- Sugar - 2 tbsps.
- Salt - ½ tsp.

Procedure:

1. Add apples into a pan, then cook over heat.
2. Next, add sugar and cook until the apples get caramelized.
3. Add cinnamon stick, chili powder, and salt and mix. Cook for 15 minutes.
4. Using a blender, process the chutney after cooling.
5. Pour chutney into a clean jar.
6. You can serve or store.

Nutrition per serving: Calories 53 | Fat 0.2 g | Carbs 14 g | Sugar 10.9 g | Protein 0.3 g

10.7.4 Cranberry Chutney

Serves: 4 | Preparation time: 10 mins | Cooking Time: 10 mins

Ingredients:

- Cranberries - 12 oz.
- Brown sugar - ½ c.
- Orange juice - 1
- Whole-grain mustard - 1 tsp.
- Vinegar - ¼ c.
- Peeled & diced apple - 1
- Grated fresh ginger - 1 tsp.
- Minced onion - ½
- Olive oil - 1 tbsp.
- Salt - ½ tsp.

Procedure:

1. Add oil to a pan over heat.
2. Saute the ginger, onion, and apple for 3 minutes.
3. Add the remaining ingredients, then continue cooking for about 10 minutes.
4. Pour chutney into a clean jar after cooling.
5. You can serve or store.

Nutrition per serving: Calories 195 | Fat 3.7 g | Carbs 37.3 g | Sugar 28.9 g | Protein 0.5 g

10.7.5 Rhubarb Chutney

Serves: 6-pint jars | Preparation time: 5 mins | Cooking Time: 20 mins

Ingredients:

- Sliced rhubarb - 8 c.
- Sliced onion - 6 c.
- Raisins - 2 c.
- Light brown sugar - 7 c.
- Ground cloves - 1 tsp.
- Apple cider vinegar - 4 c.
- Salt - 2 tbsps.
- Cayenne pepper - 1/8 tsp.
- Cinnamon - 2 tsps.
- Ginger - 2 tsps.

Procedure:

1. Mix your fixings in a pot, let boil, then simmer gently until the liquid gets slightly thickened. Pour into sterile jars and wipe the rims.
2. Tighten the lids, then set your jars in a water bath canner, process for 10 minutes.
3. Finally, cool before you store.

Nutrition per serving: Calories 58 | Fat 1 g | Carbs 12 g | Protein 0 g

10.7.6 Plum Chutney

Serves: 5 half pint jars | Preparation time: 15 mins | Cooking Time: 60 mins

Ingredients:

- Lightly packed brown sugar - 1 c.
- Chopped pitted red plums - 4 c.
- Chopped crystallized ginger - ½ c.
- Mustard seed - 1 tbsp.
- Chopped onion - 1
- Pickling salt - ½ tsp.
- Chopped raisins - ½ c.
- Red pepper flakes - 1 tsp.
- Apple cider vinegar - 2 c.

Procedure:

1. In your pot over heat, combine the plums, onion, raisins, ginger, mustard seed, pepper flakes, salt, vinegar, and brown sugar.
2. Boil, then reduce the heat and simmer for 1 hour. Ensure that you stir the mixture occasionally.
3. Pack the chutney into 5 clean ½-pint jars, leaving ½" headspace. Close with lids.
4. Finally, set in a water bath canner, then process for 10 minutes.
5. You can serve or store it after cooling.

Nutrition per serving: Calories 60 | Fat 0 g | Carbs 13 g | Protein 0 g

10.7.7 Jalapeno-Pear Chutney

Serves: 5 half pint jars | Preparation time: 15 mins | Cooking Time: 45 mins

Ingredients:

- Cider vinegar - 1 c.
- Ground mustard - 1 tsp.
- Peeled and chopped pears - 2 lbs.
- Packed brown sugar - 1 c.
- Peeled, seeded, and chopped tomatoes - 2 lbs.
- Chopped onions - 2 c.
- Finely chopped seeded jalapeno peppers - 1 c.
- Minced fresh ginger root - 4 tsps.
- Crushed red pepper - 1 tsp.

Procedure:

1. In a Dutch oven, combine the ingredients. Boil.

2. Next, reduce temperature, then simmer for 60 minutes, uncovered as you stir after some time.
3. Ladle hot mixture into hot half-pint jars, leaving ½" headspace.
4. Finally, set your jars in a water bath, then process for 10 minutes.
5. You can serve or store it after cooling.

Nutrition per serving: Calories 71 | Fat 0.3 g | Carbs 17.3 g | Protein 0.8 g

10.7.8 Coconut Chutney

Serves: 1 | Preparation time: 15 mins | Cooking Time: 15 mins

Ingredients:

- Chopped fresh red chili peppers - 3
- Vegetable oil - 1 tbsp.
- Mustard seed - ½ tsp.
- Plain yogurt - ½ c.
- Grated fresh whole coconut - ½
- Cumin seeds - ¼ tsp.

Procedure:

1. Process together yogurt and coconut to a fine paste; transfer to a bowl.
2. Cook chili, cumin, and mustard in oil in a skillet until the seeds start popping. Next, pour the seed combination into the coconut mixture.
3. Finally, mix thoroughly.
4. Enjoy.

10.7.9 Delicious Bourbon Bacon Chutney

Serves: 4 | Preparation time: 10 mins | Cooking Time: 45 mins

Ingredients:

- Bourbon - ½ c.
- Chopped red onions - 2
- Butter - 2 tbsps.
- Chopped bacon slices - 12
- Minced garlic cloves - 3

Procedure:

1. Add bacon when the pan is hot, then cook for 10 minutes.
2. Then reduce the temperature, adding butter, garlic, and onions.

3. Cook for 20 minutes, then add the bourbon cooking the mixture for 15 minutes as you stir occasionally.
4. Serve.

Nutrition per serving: Calories 24 | Fat 18 g | Carbs 9 g | Protein 6 g

10.7.10 Tangy Mango Chutney

Serves: 6-pint jars | Preparation time: 10 mins | Cooking Time: 20 mins

Ingredients:

- Red pepper flakes - ¼ tsp.
- Diced onion - ½ c.
- Salt - ½ tsp.
- Golden raisins - ¾ c.
- Diced red bell pepper - ½ c.
- Freshly grated ginger - 1 tbsp.
- Granulated sugar - 2 c.
- Apple cider vinegar - ½ c.
- Diced mangoes - 6 c.

Procedure:

1. Mix the ingredients in a saucepan. Next, boil, reduce the heat, then simmer the mixture for 20 minutes once it has reached a rolling boil. The mixture should become more viscous as it cools. Don't forget to give it a little stir now and then.
2. If the chutney is too thick, do the freezer test: Put a dish in the freezer, then add a tiny bit of chutney.
3. Run a spoon through it once it gets frozen for two minutes. Chutney gets finished if it doesn't smoosh together. You may try again if the chutney doesn't split when you run a spoon through it by reheating it for a few minutes.
4. Your chutney is ready to be stored in jars. Ensure that there is enough headspace in your jars before sealing and tightening.
5. Check to see whether the water n your canner is at a boil. Place the jars one at a time and monitor the water level as you go. You want to cover the jars all the way. Re-boil the water, cover the pot, and set a 10-minute timer.

Nutrition per serving: Calories 33 | Fat 0.1 g | Carbs 8.3 g | Protein 0.1 g

10.8 JELLIES

10.8.1 Jasmine Tea Jelly

Serves: 6 half pint jars | Preparation time: 15 mins | Cooking Time: 12 mins

Ingredients:

- Water - 4 c.
- Minced fresh ginger - 1 tbsp.
- Jasmine green tea - ¼ c.
- Powdered fruit pectin - 1.75 oz.
- Lemon juice - ¼ c.
- Sugar - 5 c.

Procedure:

1. Mix the water and ginger in a saucepan. Boil, then reduce the heat, and simmer for 5 minutes, covered.
2. Next, stir in the jasmine green tea. Cover, then boil for 5 minutes.
3. Sieve the ginger mixture and discard the solids. Take 3½ c. of the liquid and transfer it to a saucepan.
4. Stir in the fruit pectin and lemon juice, and boil for 2 minutes.
5. Next, pour in the sugar, then boil for 1 minute as you stir constantly.
6. Next, skim off the foam, and ladle it into your sterilized jars, leaving ¼" headspace.
7. Close with the lid, then set the jars in a water canner, then process for 10 minutes.
8. You can serve or store it after cooling.

Nutrition per serving: Calories 44 | Fat 0 g | Carbs 12 g | Protein 2 g

10.8.2 Jalapeño Pepper Jelly

Serves: 5 half pint jars | Preparation time: 10 mins | Cooking Time: 5 mins

Ingredients:

- Chopped jalapeño pepper - 1/3 c.
- Sugar - 4 c.
- Cider vinegar - 1 c.
- Chopped green bell pepper - 1 c.

- Pectin - 6 oz.

Procedure:

1. Mix all the fixings in a saucepot, then boil for about 5 minutes. Let it cool within 1 hour, and then put them into jars.
2. Set the jars for 5 minutes in a water bath, then stand for a minimum of 12 hours before storing.

Nutrition per serving: Calories 651 | Fat 26 g | Carbs 93 g | Protein 17 g

10.8.3 Cranberry Orange Jelly

Serves: 6 half pint jars | Preparation time: 15 mins | Cooking Time: 5 mins

Ingredients:

- Unsweetened cranberry juice - 3½ c.
- Powdered pectin - 1.75 oz.
- Granulated sugar - 5 c.
- Grated orange zest - 1

Procedure:

1. In a pot over heat, combine the cranberry juice and pectin. Boil the mixture as you stir.
2. Add the sugar, stirring until it dissolves. Next, add the orange zest.
3. Boil the mixture as you stir constantly.
4. Next, skim off the foam.
5. Ladle into 6 clean half-pint jars, leaving ¼" headspace. Top with 2-piece lids and rings and close until finger-tight.
6. Set in a water bath canner for 10 minutes.
7. You can serve or store it after cooling.

Nutrition per serving: Calories 202 | Fat 2.3 g | Carbs 31.4 g | Protein 14.8 g

10.8.4 Cucumber Jelly

Serves: 8 half pint jars | Preparation time: 20 mins | Cooking Time: 10 mins

Ingredients:

- 7 c. sugar

- 1 c. vinegar
- 2 ½ c. cucumber juice, strained
- Seeds scraped from one vanilla bean.
- 2 pouches pectin

Procedure:

1. Combine the cucumber juice, sugar, vinegar, and seeds in a pot and boil as you stir often.
2. Next, pull from the heat after boiling for an extra 2 minutes.
3. Return to a boil with the pectin for 2 minutes, stirring occasionally.
4. Next, skim off the foam.
5. Fill hot sterilized ½-pint jars with jelly, leaving a ¼" headspace.
6. Next, place caps on jars, then screw on bands.
7. Finally, set your jars in a hot water bath, then process for 10 minutes.
8. You can serve or store it after cooling.

Nutrition per serving: Calories 35 | Fat 0 g | Carbs 25 g | Protein 0 g

10.8.5 Bell Pepper Jelly

Serves: 3¼ pint jars | Preparation time: 15 mins | Cooking Time: 10 mins

Ingredients:

- Cider vinegar - 2/3 c.
- Finely chopped and seeded green bell pepper - 2 1/3 c.
- Pectin - 3 tbsps.
- Butter - ½ tsp.
- finely chopped cleaned jalapeño pepper - 1/3 c.
- Sugar - 3 1/3 c.

Procedure:

1. Place pectin and peppers in a bowl, then pour vinegar over them. Next, add butter, then stir the mixture before adding sugar and pectin.
2. Boil for 4 minutes.
3. Next, pour the mixture into jars, leaving ¼" from the top. Screw the lids after placing them on top of the jars.
4. Set your jars in a boiling water bath, then process for 10 minutes.
5. You can serve or store it after cooling.

Nutrition per serving: Calories 32 | Fat 0 g | Carbs 8 g | Protein 1 g

10.8.6 Grapes Jelly

Serves: 4 half pint jars | Preparation time: 15 mins | Cooking Time: 25 mins

Ingredients:

- Grapes with stems removed - 3 c.
- Sugar - 3 c.
- Lemon juice - 2 tbsps.
- Water – 3 c.

Procedure:

1. In a bowl, mash the grapes. Next, add the water and boil the mixture as you stir frequently.
2. Simmer for 10 minutes after reducing the heat.
3. Strain the juice through a fine-meshed strainer.
4. Transfer the juice to a saucepan, leaving the sediment and 3 c. of sugar. Boil for 10 minutes as you stir.
5. Next, pour in the lemon juice, and remove and skim off the foam. Ladle the grape jelly into jars, leaving ¼" of headspace.
6. Close your jars, place them in a water bath canner, cover with the lid, and process for 10 minutes.
7. You can serve or store it after cooling.

Nutrition per serving: Calories 86 | Fat 0.1 g | Carbs 7 g | Protein 2 g

10.8.7 Dandelion Jelly

Serves: 3-pint jars | Preparation time: 15 mins | Cooking Time: 15 mins

Ingredients:

- Yellow parts of dandelion blossoms - 4 c.
- Boiling water - 3 c.
- Granulated sugar - 4½ c.
- Yellow food coloring - 20 drops
- Fresh lemon juice - 2 tbsps.
- Powdered fruit pectin - 3-oz.

Procedure:

1. In your saucepan, mix the flowers and water. Next, simmer the mixture for 10 minutes.

2. Next, ensure you strain the water. Make sure your final measure is 3 c. of juice.
3. Return juice to your saucepan and boil. Next, add sugar, food coloring, and lemon juice before you add the pectin. Follow by boilig the mixture for about 1 minute.
4. Pour hot jelly into sterilized jars, leaving ¼" headspace at the top of each jar.
5. Finally, process for 10 minutes in a water-bath canner after tightening the lids.
6. You can serve or store it after cooling.

Nutrition per serving: Calories 28 | Fat 0 g | Carbs 4.4 g | Protein 0.1 g

10.8.8 Root Beer Jelly

Serves: 2½ pint jars | Preparation time: 10 mins | Cooking Time: 3 mins

Ingredients:

- Root beer - 1 c.
- Granulated sugar - 3 c.
- Water - ½ c.
- Liquid pectin bottle - ½

Procedure:

1. Combine the ingredients, reserving pectin.
2. Boil. Next, add pectin, stirring constantly, and hard boil for 30 seconds.
3. Next, ladle into jars.
4. Set the jars in water bath canner, then process for 5 minutes.
5. You can serve or store it after cooling.

Nutrition per serving: Calories 170 | Fat 0 g | Carbs 47 g | Protein 0 g

10.8.9 Garlic Jelly

Serves: 6-pint jars | Preparation time: 15 mins | Cooking Time: 5 mins

Ingredients:

- Divided white vinegar - 2 c.
- Granulated sugar - 5 c.
- Peeled garlic - ¼ lb.
- Liquid fruit pectin - 3 oz.

Procedure:

1. In your food processor, blend garlic and ½ c. vinegar.
2. In a stockpot over heat, mix garlic mixture, sugar, and remaining vinegar. Boil the mixture as you stir constantly.
3. Next, stir in pectin, and return to a boil. Finally, boil hard for 1 minute as you stir constantly.
4. Next, ladle hot jelly into sterilized jars, leaving ¼" headspace at the top of each jar.
5. Process in a water-bath canner for 10 minutes after tightening the lids.
6. You can serve or store it after cooling.

Nutrition per serving: Calories 23 | Fat 0 g | Carbs 4.5 g | Protein 0.2 g

10.9 RELISH

10.9.1 Radish Relish

Serves: 32 | Preparation time: 10 mins | Cooking Time: 30 mins

Ingredients:

- Stemmed radishes - 3 c.
- Prepared horseradish - 2 tbsps.
- Vinegar - 1 c.
- Mustard seeds - 1 tbsp.
- Sugar - 1 c.
- Onion - 1
- Celery ribs - 2
- Salt - 2 tsps.

Procedure:

1. Finely chop the radishes, onion, and celery. Next, add to a bowl. Pour in the remaining ingredients, then mix. Consider leaving it to sit for 3 hours.
2. Transfer vegetable mixture into the saucepan and boil for 10 minutes.
3. Ladle vegetable mixture into the jars. Leave ½" headspace.
4. Seal jars with lids, then process for 20 minutes in a boiling water bath.
5. You can serve or store it after cooling.

Nutrition per serving: Calories 30 | Fat 0.1 g | Carbs 7.2 g | Sugar 6.7 g | Protein 0.2 g

10.9.2 Jalapeno Relish

Serves: 12 | Preparation time: 10 mins | Cooking Time: 45 mins

Ingredients:

- Chopped jalapenos - 2 lb.
- Sugar - 6 tsps.
- Water - 1½ c.
- Vinegar - 3 c.
- Oregano - 2 tbsps.
- Minced garlic cloves - 4
- Chopped onion - 1

- Chopped tomatoes - 2 lb.
- Salt - 6 tsps.

Procedure:

1. Add the ingredients into a bowl and mix. Next, let sit for 10 minutes.
2. Ladle vegetable mixture into the jars. Leave ½" headspace.
3. Seal jars with lids, then process for 45 minutes in a boiling water bath.
4. You can serve or store it after cooling.

Nutrition per serving: Calories 64 | Fat 0.7 g | Carbs 11.6 g | Sugar 7.3 g | Protein 1.8 g

10.9.3 Corn Relish

Serves: 16 | Preparation time: 10 mins | Cooking Time: 60 mins

Ingredients:

- Husked & cleaned corn ears - 8
- Mustard seed - 1 tsp.
- Celery seed - 1 tsp.
- Apple cider vinegar - 2 c.
- Sugar - 1 c.
- Chopped onion - 1 c.
- Chopped cucumber - ½
- Chopped red bell pepper - ¾ c.
- Chopped green bell peppers - 1½ c.
- Peeled, seeded, & chopped tomatoes - 2 lb.
- Salt - 1 tbsp.

Procedure:

1. Cut corn from the cobs.
2. In a saucepan, mix corn, onion, cucumbers, bell peppers, and tomatoes.
3. In another saucepan, mix sugar, vinegar, celery seed, mustard seed, and salt, and pour over the vegetable mixture. Boil, then simmer for 60 minutes.
4. Finally, ladle the relish in a clean jar.
5. You can serve or store it after cooling.

Nutrition per serving: Calories 141 | Fat 1.2 g | Carbs 31.9 g | Sugar 17.9 g | Protein 3.4 g

10.9.4 Green Tomato Relish

Serves: 10 | Preparation time: 10 mins | Cooking Time: 30 mins

Ingredients:

- Sliced green tomatoes - 8 c.
- Celery seeds - ½ tsp.
- Mustard seeds - 3 tbsps.
- Sugar - 2 c.
- Vinegar - 2 c.
- Chopped hot red pepper - 1
- Chopped sweet red peppers - 2
- Sliced onion - 3 c.
- Turmeric - ½ tsp.
- Salt - 1 tsp.

Procedure:

1. In a bowl, add green tomatoes and salt. Cover and let sit overnight.
2. In a pot, mix the vinegar, onions, turmeric, celery seeds, mustard seeds, and sugar. Stir, then boil. Next, simmer for 5 minutes.
3. Drain tomatoes. Add green tomatoes and peppers to the vinegar mixture and boil. Next, simmer for 20 minutes.
4. Ladle relish into the clean jars.
5. You can serve or store it after cooling.

Nutrition per serving: Calories 225 | Fat 1.5 g | Carbs 52 g | Sugar 47 g | Protein 2.8 g

10.9.5 Jalapeno Pepper Relish

Serves: 8-pint jars | Preparation time: 15 mins | Cooking Time: 25 mins

Ingredients:

- Chopped jalapeño peppers - 5 lb.
- Sugar - 2 c.
- White vinegar - 4 c.
- Cilantro leaves - ½ c.

Procedure:

1. In a food processor, slice the peppers.
2. In a pot, stir the sugar into the vinegar and boil.
3. In your food processor, slice the cilantro leaves, then stir them into your peppers.

4. Ladle the uncooked peppers and cilantro into your canning jars, then spoon the liquid over the mixture, allowing ½" headspace.
5. Set the jars in a water bath canner for 10 minutes.
6. You can serve or store it after cooling.

Nutrition per serving: Calories 36 | Fat 0 g | Carbs 10 g | Protein 0 g

10.9.6 Beet Relish

Serves: 4-pint jars | Preparation time: 20 mins | Cooking Time: 10 mins

Ingredients:

- Chopped cabbage - 4 c.
- Sugar - 1½ c.
- Chopped sweet red pepper - 1 c.
- Pickling salt - 1 tbsp.
- Horseradish - 1 tbsp.
- Cooked chopped beets - 4 c.
- Chopped onion - 1 c.
- White vinegar - 3 c.

Procedure:

1. Combine the ingredients in a pot. Simmer for 10 minutes. Boil, then pack hot into hot jars, ensuring that you reserve ¼" headspace.
2. Tighten the lids.
3. Finally, place in a bath canner with boiling water and process for 15 minutes.
4. You can serve or store it after cooling.

Nutrition per serving: Calories 34 | Fat 0 g | Carbs 8 g | Protein 0 g

10.9.7 Cranberry Raspberry Relish

Serves: 2-pint jars | Preparation time: 20 mins | Cooking Time: 40 mins

Ingredients:

- Fresh cranberries - 4 c.
- Finely chopped crystallized ginger - ¾ c.
- White sugar - ½ c.
- Raspberries - 3 c.
- Red wine vinegar - 1 c.

Procedure:

1. Combine the fixings in a saucepan and boil. Next, lower the heat and simmer for 40 minutes.
2. Ladle into sterilized jars, leaving about a ¼" headspace.
3. Finally, set in a water bath, then process for 15 minutes.
4. You can serve or store it after cooling.

Nutrition per serving: Calories 58 | Fat 0.2 g | Carbs 14.7 g | Protein 0.4 g

10.9.8 Citrus Cucumber & Strawberry Relish

Serves: 4 | Preparation time: 20 mins | Cooking Time: 5 mins

Ingredients

- Chopped English cucumber - 1 c.
- Orange juice - 1 tbsp.
- Lime juice - 2 tbsps.
- Chopped fresh strawberries - 1 c.
- Chopped cilantro - 1 tbsp.
- Chopped jalapeño pepper - 2 tbsps.
- Lime zest - 1 tsp.
- Coarsely chopped oranges - 2
- Honey - 1 tsp.
- Chopped red onion - 1 c.
- Kosher salt - ½ tsp.

Procedure:

1. Combine the ingredients in a bowl.
2. Next, let it stand for10 minutes before you serve.

Nutrition per serving: Calories 60 | Fat 0.3 g | Carbs 14.9 g | Sugar 11 g | Protein 1.2 g | Sodium 242 mg

10.9.9 Lemon Jalapeno & Cranberry Relish

Serves: 8 | Preparation time: 10 mins | Cooking Time: 20 mins

Ingredients:

- Cranberries - 1½ c.
- Extra-virgin olive oil - 2 tbsps.
- Lime juice - 2 tsps.
- Chopped fresh jalapeños - 2
- Lime zest - 1 tsp.
- Sugar - ⅓ c.
- Minced red onion - 2 tbsps.
- Salt - ½ tsp.

Procedure:

1. Process the ingredients in a food processor.
2. You can serve or store it in a refrigerator.

Nutrition per serving: Calories 85 | Fat 3.6 g | Carbs 14 g | Sugar 10 g | Protein 0.2 g | Sodium 19 mg

11 PRESSURE CANNING RECIPES

11.1 VEGETABLES

11.1.1 Simple Butternut Squash

Serves: 1 pint | Prep Time: 1 ½ hour | Cook Time: 1 ½ hour

Ingredients:

- Butternut squash - 1
- Water – 1 ½ c.

Procedure:

1. Remove the stem and seeds from the butternut squash before washing and peeling them. Ideally, the cubes are 3 centimeters in size (1 inch). Squash cubes should be blanched in boiling water for two minutes.
2. Using a ladle, transfer the mixture to half- or one-liter (US quart) jars. 2. Allow a 3 cm headroom (1 inch).
3. Overfilling a container with hot, clean water can help keep the headspace intact (from a kettle, for example).
4. Headspace should be reduced and re-aligned.
5. Wipe the jar's rims clean.
6. The containers should now be sealed with the lids.
7. When it comes to pressure, the dial and weighted gauges are the same at 10 lbs. and 11 pounds, respectively (76 kPa) For altitudes higher than 300 meters (1000 feet), the pressure should be lowered.
8. A 1-liter (us quart) jar takes 90 minutes to process whereas a half-liter may be processed in 55 minutes.

Nutrition per serving: Calories 83 | Carbs 24 g | Protein: 2.1 g. | Sodium: 33 mg | Fat: 0.2 g,

11.1.2 Asparagus

Serves: 4 quarts | Prep Time: 15 minutes | Cook Time: 40 minutes

Ingredients:

- Asparagus - 14 lbs.
- Salt - 4 tsps.

Procedure:

1. Clean the asparagus and snap off tough ends and cut into 6-inch pieces.
2. Lay the jar on the stand de, and slide asparagus in with the wide base toward the bottom. Keep adding asparagus until you can't. Add 1tsp salt to each quart jar.
3. Pour boiling water into the jars. Process them at 10 lbs. pressure for 40 minutes, or 11 lbs. with a dial gauge canner.
4. Let cool for 12 hours and remove.

Nutrition per serving: Calories: 87 Fat: 1 g Carbs: 16 g Protein: 10 g

11.1.3 Eggplant Appetizer

Serves: 1 | Prep Time: 10 Minutes | Cook Time: 1 Hour 40 minutes

Ingredients:

- diced parsley - ¼ c.
- water - ¼ c.
- crushed basil - ¼ tsp.
- green pepper, chopped - ½ c.
- chopped onion - ½ c.
- crushed oregano - ½ tsp.
- mushroom stems and pieces - 1 can
- canned tomato paste - 1 c.
- red wine vinegar - 1 c.
- eggplant, sliced into small cubes - 1
- sugar - 1 tbsp.
- kosher salt - 1 tsp.
- minced garlic - 2 cloves
- olive oil - 2 tbsps.
- Black pepper – ¼ tsp.

Procedure:

1. Heat the oil and the garlic in a large skillet. Add the eggplant, mushroom, green pepper, onion, and parsley and toss together to mix. Close and cook on low for 10 minutes.
2. In a medium skillet, stir together the sugar, oregano, basil, salt, and pepper. Add the tomato paste, water, and vinegar. Include the eggplant mixture in the skillet and stir in the remaining ingredients.
3. Cover and let it cook gently until the eggplant is tender.
4. Pour this into sterile jars, remove the air bubbles and fill to a ½ inch headspace. Clean the jar rims clean and adjusts the lids.

Nutrition per serving: Calories 204| Carbs 16.3 g| Protein: 1.3 g| Sodium: 43 mg| Fat: 4.1 g,

11.1.4 Sweet Carrots

Serves: 4 pints | Prep Time: 10 minutes | Cook Time: 28 minutes

Ingredients:

- water - 1 c.
- sugar - 2 c.
- canning salt - 2 tsps.
- pickling spice - 3 tbsps.
- white distilled vinegar 5% - 5 ½ c.
- peeled carrots - 8 ½ c.

Procedure:

1. Wash and peel the tiny carrots, if preferred, and place them in a bowl.
2. Using a large stockpot, allow the remaining ingredients to boil for about 3 minutes.
3. Allow the mixture to boil, then add carrots. Cook at a simmer for about 10 minutes, or until the pasta is half-cooked. Then you may get rid of it.
4. Carrots should be poured into jars with a 1-inch headspace. Leave half-inch headroom at the top of the container.
5. Process for 15 minutes and make altitude adjustments
6. Remove the ice cubes after ½ hour.

Nutrition per serving: Calories: 557 Carbs 125 g Protein: 2 g Sodium: 1,389 mg, Potassium: 691 mg Sugar: 1½ g

11.1.5 Veggie Chili Recipe

Serves: 8 pints | Preparation Time 20 minutes | Cook Time: 20 minutes

Ingredients:

- chopped onion - 1 c.
- canned tomatoes - 1 pint
- pepper - 1/4 tsp.
- cumin - 1/4 tsp.
- minced garlic - 2 cloves
- dry beans - 2 lbs.
- salt - 2 tbsps.
- chili powder - 6 tbsps.
- boiling water - 7 c.

Procedure:

1. After washing and rinsing the beans, let them soak overnight. Drain. The water and all the other ingredients should be boiled for five minutes.
2. Leave a half-inch of headroom when filling the hot sterilized jars with the mixture Get rid of any lingering bubbles of air.
3. Use a clean jar rim to tighten the bands around the jar lid (do not screw too tightly).
4. Use a pressure canner set to 11 lbs. (dial) or 10 lbs. (weight) and process the jars for 75 minutes. Adapt to the altitude if you need to. After dropping the pressure to zero, wait 10 minutes.
5. You should wait for at least 12 to 24 hours before you open your jars to ensure that the lids don't drop down or pop up. Keep in a cool, dark place.

Nutrition per serving: Calories 339| Protein 21 g| Carbs 12 g

11.1.6 Parsnips

Serves: 1 pint | Prep Time: 20 minutes | Cook Time: 40 minutes

Ingredients:

- parsnips - ½ lbs.
- Salt – ¼ tsp.
- Water – 2 c.

Procedure:

1. Cut the parsnips into two-inch slices after they have been well washed. Afterward, blanch for four minutes in hot water before plunging into cold water to ensure cooking process stops.
2. Fill jars halfway with parsnips, then top with 1 inch of boiling water. You may choose to add salt to your meal if desired.
3. Using a dial gauge, apply 10 lbs. pressure to the jars for 30 minutes.
4. Wait at least 12-24 hours before removing it from the oven.

Nutrition per serving: Calories: 75 Fibers: 4 g Carbs: 24 g Fat: 0.5 g

11.1.7 Asparagus Spears

Serves: 2 | Prep Time: 10 Minutes | Cook Time: 1 Hour

Ingredients:

- 10 tbsps. salt.
- 16 lbs. of asparagus spears.
- Boiling water – 4 c.

Procedure:

1. Bring a large saucepan of water to a boil, then add the asparagus and salt to taste. 3 minutes of boiling time.
2. In sterilized jars, fill in asparagus and liquid to the brim leaving 1-inch headspace.
3. Set in a pressure can and process your jars for 30 minutes using a weighted gauge at 10 lbs. of pressure or an 11-lb. dial gauge at 11 lbs. of pressure.

Nutrition per serving: Calories 104| Sodium: 33 mg, Dietary Fiber: 1.4 g| Fat: 4.1 g| Carbs 16.3 g| Protein: 1.3 g.

11.1.8 Cubed White Potatoes

Serves: 9 | Prep Time: 20 minutes | Cook Time: 45 minutes

Ingredients:

- Potatoes, 13 lbs.
- Salt, 4 tbsps.
- Boiling water
- Lemon juice – 1 c.

Procedure:

1. Rinse and peel the potatoes and put them in a solution of lemon juice and 1 gallon of water to keep them from becoming brown.
2. Cook the potatoes for 10 minutes in salted boiling water, then drain. Paper towels may be used to drain them.
3. Fill the sterilized jars with the potatoes and seal them. Allow a 1-inch headroom by filling the saucepan with new hot water.
4. For pressure canners with a weighted gauge, or dial gauge canners, the process for 35 minutes at 10 lbs. of pressure or 11 lbs. of pressure.

Nutrition per serving: Calories 117 Calories| Fat: 0.1 g| Sodium: 539 mg| Carbs 17 g| Protein: 14.2 g

11.1.9 Canned Carrots

Serve: 14 | Prep Time: 10 minutes | Cook Time: 30 minutes

Ingredients:

- carrots, wash, peel & sliced 1 ½-inch thick - 14 lbs
- Water – 7 c.
- Salt – 1 tsp.

Procedure:

1. Pack carrots into the clean jars. Leave a headspace of 1-inch.
2. To each of the quart jars, add 1 tsp salt.
3. Top the carrots with boiling water. Leave headspace of 1-inch.
4. Add lids and your rings. Place jar into the pressure canner.
5. Process can carrots: quarts for 30 minutes, pints for 25 minutes at 10 lbs pressure in a pressure canner.
6. Once done, cool canner, remove lid and allow jars to stand for 10 minutes before removing from canner.

7. Remove carrot jars from the canner and place them on a countertop for 12 hours.
8. Check seals of jars. Label and store.

Nutrition per serving: Calories 186 | Fat 0 g | Carbs 44.6 g | Sugar 22.3 g | Protein 3.7 g | Cholesterol 0 mg

11.1.10   Canned Potatoes

Serve: 12 | Prep Time: 10 minutes | Cook Time: 35 minutes

Ingredients:

- potatoes, clean & cut into 2-inch pieces - 6 lbs.
- Water – 4 c.

Procedure:

1. Add potatoes into the pot and cover with water. Allow to boil, reduce heat intensity, and cook for about 10 minutes.
2. Drain potatoes well.
3. Pack potatoes in a clean jar. Pour hot water over potatoes. Leave a headspace of 1-inch.
4. Add lids and rings. Place jar into the pressure canner.
5. Process can potatoes: pints for 35 minutes, quarts for 40 minutes at 10 lbs pressure in a pressure canner.
6. Once done, cool canner, remove lid and allow the jars to stand for about 10 minutes before removing from canner.
7. Remove potatoes jars from the canner and set them on a countertop for 1-2 hours.
8. Check seals of jars. Label and store.

Nutrition per serving: Calories 156 | Fat 0.2 g | Carbs 35.6 g | Sugar 2.6 g | Protein 3.8 g | Cholesterol 0 mg

11.1.11 Canned Sweet Potatoes

Serve: 12 | Prep Time: 10 minutes | Cook Time: 1 hour 30 minutes

Ingredients:

- sweet potatoes, peel & diced into 1 1/2-inch piece - 6 lbs
- sugar - 2 ¼ c.
- water - 5 ¼ c.

Procedure:

1. using a saucepan, add in water and sugar and allow to boil. Reduce heat and simmer until sugar is dissolved.
2. Pack sweet potatoes into the clean jars then pour hot sugar syrup to the sweet potatoes. Leave a headspace of 1-inch.
3. Add lids and rings. Place jar into the pressure canner.
4. Process can sweet potatoes: quarts for 1 hour 30 minutes at 10 lbs pressure in a pressure canner.
5. Once done, cool canner, remove your lid and allow the jars to stand for about 10 minutes before removing from canner.
6. Remove sweet potato jars from canner and place them on the counter for 2-4 hours.
7. Check seals of jars. Label and store.

Nutrition per serving: Calories 408 | Fat 0.4 g | Carbs 100.7 g | Sugar 38.6 g | Protein 3.5 g | Cholesterol 0 mg

11.1.12   Canned Zucchini

Serve: 6 | Prep Time: 10 minutes | Cook Time: 10 minutes

Ingredients:

- zucchini, cut into ¼-inch thick slices - 3 lbs
- black peppercorns - 5
- bay leaves - 2
- vinegar - 1 c.
- sugar - 1 c.
- water - 8 c.
- sliced red pepper - 1
- dill sprigs - 4
- baby carrots, cut into strips - 12
- garlic cloves - 3
- sliced onions - 2
- tomatoes - 1 ½ lbs.
- salt - 2 ½ tbsps.

Procedure:

1. Using a pot, add sugar, vinegar, water, and salt and allow to boil.

2. Evenly divide peppercorns, bay leaves, red pepper, dill sprigs, carrots, cloves, onions, tomatoes, and salt into the jars.
3. Pack zucchini into the jars. Remove air bubbles.
4. Use lids to seal jars and process for 10 minutes in a boiling water bath.
5. Take jars from water bath and allow to cool completely.
6. Check seals of jars. Label and store.

Nutrition per serving: Calories 215 | Fat 0.8 g | Carbs 51.6 g | Sugar 43.4 g | Protein 4.4 g | Cholesterol 0 mg

11.1.13   Canned Okra

Serve: 8 | Prep Time: 10 minutes | Cook Time: 6 minutes

Ingredients:

- chopped okra - 8 c.
- apple cider vinegar - 8 tbsps.
- Water
- sea salt - 1 ½ tbsp

Procedure:

1. Add water, apple cider vinegar, and salt in a saucepan and bring to boil.
2. Add okra and cook for 6 minutes.
3. Remove pan from heat. Add okra into the clean jars then pour the hot liquid to top the okra. Leave a headspace of ½-inch.
4. Seal jar with lid and store in the refrigerator.

Nutrition per serving: Calories 43 | Fat 0.2 g | Carbs 7.6 g | Sugar 1.5 g | Protein 1.9 g | Cholesterol 0 mg

11.1.14   Canned Tomatoes

Serve: 8 | Prep Time: 15 minutes | Cook Time: 60 minutes

Ingredients:

- Fresh and peeled tomatoes - 15 lbs
- Fresh lemon juice – 2 tbsps.
- Salt – ½ tsp.
- Water

Procedure:

1. Add tomatoes in a large pot and cover with water. Bring to boil.
2. Boil tomatoes for 5-7 minutes. Stir frequently.
3. Add 2 tbsps. of lemon juice and 1/2 tsp. of salt to each jar.
4. Pack tomatoes in jars then top with the hot liquid. Leave a headspace of 1/2-inch.
5. Seal jars with lids and process for 40 minutes in a boiling water bath.
6. Remove the jars from the water bath and allow to cool completely.
7. Check seals of jars. Label and store.

Nutrition per serving: Calories 135 | Fat 1.5 g | Carbs 29 g | Sugar 20 g | Protein 6.7 g | Cholesterol 0 mg

11.1.15   Canned Beets

Serve: 6 | Prep Time: 10 minutes | Cook Time: 1 hour 20 minutes

Ingredients:

- beets, wash & trim stems - 10 lbs
- Water

Procedure:

1. Add beets and water in a stockpot. Boil beets until tender, about 30 minutes.
2. Once boiling done them rinse beets in cold water. Drain, cool, and peel.
3. Pack beets into clean jars. Leave a headspace of 1-inch.
4. Pour boiling water over beets. Leave a headspace of 1-inch. Remove the air bubbles.
5. Add lids and rings. Place jars into the pressure canner.
6. Process can beets: pints for 30 minutes, quarts for 35 minutes at 10 lbs pressure in a pressure canner.
7. Allow to cool canner, remove lids, and allow the jars to stand for 10 minutes before removing from canner.
8. Remove beet jars from canner and place it on the counter for 2-3 hours.
9. Check seals of jars. Label and store.

Nutrition per serving: Calories 335 | Fat 1.5 g | Carbs 75 g | Sugar 60 g | Protein 12 g | Cholesterol 0 mg

11.1.16   Canned Squash

Serve: 12 | Prep Time: 10 minutes | Cook Time: 50 minutes

Ingredients:

- summer squash, cut into 1-inch cubes - 6
- Water
- Salt

Procedure:

1. Add squash and 6 c. of water into the pot and bring boil for 3-4 minutes.
2. Add squash into the clean jars. Leave a headspace of 1-inch. Add 1/4 tsp. salt into each jar.
3. Top the squash with boiling water. Leave a headspace of 1-inch. Do away with the air bubbles.
4. Add lids and rings.
5. Place jars into the power pressure cooker for 40 minutes.
6. Remove canned squash from the power pressure cooker and let it cool.
7. Check seals of jars. Label and store.

Nutrition per serving: Calories 25 | Fat 0.4 g | Carbs 5.4 g |Sugar 2.8 g | Protein 2 g | Cholesterol 0 mg

11.2 BEANS AND LEGUMES

11.2.1 Pressure canned Green peas

Serves: 3 jars | Prep Time: 25 mins | Cook Time: 35 mins

Ingredients:

- Dried peas - 1 lb.
- Non-iodized salt
- Water

Procedure:

1. Sort the peas to remove any unwanted material.
2. Beans should be added to a small saucepan that has been partially filled with water. Boil for two minutes. To soak the beans, turn off the heat and place a lid on the pot. Let the beans sit for an hour.
3. When you've finished draining the beans, give them a good clean with plenty of fresh water. Put them back in the pan and lightly cover them with water. Over high heat, cook the peas for 30 minutes.
4. Toss a half-spoon of non-iodized salt into the jars after you've transferred the peas. Leave a 1-inch gap between each jar and the rim of the cooking liquid after filling each one halfway.
5. Use a moist cloth to clean the jar rims of any prior food residue or stains before putting on the lids and rings. Your hands may be used to tighten.
6. For 40 minutes at 10 pounds, process the jars in the canner. Consult the canning instructions provided by the manufacturer.
7. Before removing the jars from the pressure canner, let them cool and depressurize.
8. Before transporting the jars to the storage room, let them sit on a rack for 24 hours.

Nutrition per serving: Calories: 21 | Carbs 3g | Protein: 0.7g | Fat: 1g

11.2.2 Canned Garlic Beans

Serves: 3 jars | Prep Time: 45 mins | Cook Time: 30 mins

Ingredients:

- Dried black beans - 2 1/4 lbs.
- diced Garlic cloves - 5
- Handful cilantro
- Salt
- Water

Procedure:

1. Sift beans to do away with any foreign matter.
2. Cover beans in about 2 inches of water in a big pan.
3. Cook over high heat for 2 minutes, until the water and beans are boiling.
4. After the beans have been removed from heat, cover them using a lid and allow them sit for an hour. Drain water from the pan when it has been removed from heat.
5. Add just enough water to just cover the ingredients. After the beans and water have been boiling for 30 minutes, add the cilantro and garlic and toss well.
6. Fill jars with beans by use of a slotted spoon, leaving a headspace of 1-inch. Add 1/2 tsp. of salt and enough cooking liquid to cover the beans in each jar, then seal the lids tightly.
7. You're ready to finish now. Just pop some bubble wrap and wipe off the lid. Then add your rings and tighten them with your hands.
8. Ten lbs. of pressure is used to process the jars for a total of 60 minutes. Depressurize the canner before removing the jars and storing them.

Nutritional facts Calories: 147 | Carbs 13g | Protein: 5g | Fat: 0g. 17.

11.2.3 Pressure Canned Chickpeas

Serves: 5-pint jars | Prep Time: 25 mins | Cook Time: 30 mins

Ingredients:

- Chickpeas - 2 1/4 lbs.
- Salt – ½ tsp.
- Water

Procedure:

1. Wash the chickpeas and cover them with water in a saucepan. Add salt. Bring them to a boil for two minutes. Remove the chickpeas from the heat and let them sit for an hour before draining.
2. Drain the chickpeas and put them in a pot with enough water to cover them. Low-temperature cooking of the chickpeas for 30 minutes is recommended. Leave a headspace of 1-inch in the jars by filling them to the halfway point. Make sure the beans are covered by adequate boiling water by adding salt to each canister.
3. Remove the air bubble by wiping the rims of the jars. Put the jars' lids and rings on.
4. Pressure can the pint jars for 60 minutes at 10 lbs. of pressure in the pressure canner.
5. When the pressure canner has depressurized, remove the jars from the canner and discard them.

Nutrition per serving: Calories: 269| Carbs 45g| Protein: 15g| Fat: 4g.

11.2.4 Canned Garlic Garbanzo Beans

Serves: 9 jars | Prep Time: 25 minutes | Cook Time: 2 minutes,

Ingredients:

- 18 garlic cloves
- 3 tbsp salt
- 6 c. garbanzo beans
- Water

Procedure:

1. To begin, fill a large stockpot with water until the beans are covered by 2 inches of water. Bring the beans to a boil for two minutes in a saucepan on the stove.
2. Afterward, let beans soak in water for an hour before serving. The beans should be packed into the jars using a slotted spoon.
3. Each jar should have two garlic cloves and a quarter-tsp. of salt added. You may add boiling water if there isn't enough cooking liquid in each of the canning jars.

4. Place the lids and rings on the jars after wiping the rims clean with a moist cloth. Pressure can the jars at 10 lbs. for 75 minutes.
5. Remove the jars from the pressure canner once it has depressurized.

Nutrition per serving: Calories 268, fat 5g, carbs 46g, Protein 15g, Sugars 7g, Fiber 13g

11.2.5 Canned Mustard Pork and Beans

Serves: 3 jars | Prep Time: 25 minutes | Cook Time: 30 minutes

Ingredients:

- salt - 1 tbsp
- yellow mustard - 1 tbsp
- brown sugar - 1/4 c.
- navy beans - 2 lbs.
- chopped onions - 2
- honey - 2 tbsp
- water - 3 c.
- tomato sauce - 30 oz.
- salt pork - 8 pieces

Procedure:

1. Preheat your pressure canner.
2. Place a half cup of navy beans in each jar. Divide the onions equally among the jars then add a piece of pork to each jar.
3. Heat a saucepan and add honey, tomato sauce, sugar, mustard, salt and water. Allow your mixture to boil. Ladle the sauce mixture to each jar.
4. Fill the jar with boiling water ensuring you leave a 1-inch headspace.
5. Wipe jar rims and place the lids and rings on the jars. Process the jars for 75 minutes at 10 lbs. of pressure in the pressure canner.
6. Remove the jars from the pressure canner when it has depressurized. For up to a year, keep in a cool, dry location.

Nutrition per serving: Calories 130, fat 1g, carbs 26g, Protein 5g, Sugars 8g, Fiber 6g| Sodium 440mg, Potassium 260mg

11.2.6 Canned Garlic Beans

Serves: 3 jars | Prep Time: 45 minutes | Cook Time: 30 minutes

Ingredients:

- dried black beans - 2 1/4 lb.
- diced garlic cloves - 5
- cilantro - handful
- Salt
- Water

Procedure:

1. Remove any unwanted substances from the beans by sorting them. Cover the beans with approximately 2 inches of water in a big pan. Allow to boil.
2. Take out the beans and let them soak for an hour with a lid on. Remove the water from the pan and return it to the stovetop.
3. Continue to top up with water until the pan is just barely submerged. Add garlic and cilantro. The beans should be boiled for around 30 minutes.
4. Make sure to leave a 1-inch headspace by using a slotted spoon to fill jars. Each jar of beans should have half a tsp. of salt added to it, followed by the cooking liquid. Using a pair of tweezers, tighten the lid and rings after removing the air bubbles.
5. The jars should be processed for 60 minutes at a pressure of 10 lbs. per square inch. Make sure the canner has depressurized completely before removing the prepared jars.

Nutrition per serving: Calories 147| Fat 0g| Carbs 13g| Protein 5g| Sodium 10

11.2.7 Canned Dry Kidney beans

Serves: 8 | Prep Time: 2 hours | Cook Time: 45 minutes

Ingredients:

- vinegar - 2 tbsp
- dried black beans - 3 lbs.
- Water

Procedure:

1. Sort beans to away with unwanted particles.
2. Using a bowl, set in beans and cover with water. Mix in vinegar and let it sit for two hours. Using a large pot, add in the beans and allow to boil before draining them. Bring 2 inches of water to a boil in a saucepan.
3. Scoop the beans into the jars, leaving a headspace of 1-inch. After filling the jars to the top, seal the lids. Allow for a 1-inch space at the top.
4. Make sure that the jars are sealed and put in a pressure canner.
5. Process at 10 lbs. of pressure for about one and a half hours and thirty minutes.
6. Allow the jars to cool fully once they have been removed from the canner. Make sure the lids are well closed before storage.

Nutrition per serving: Calories 581, fat 2.4g| Carbs 106.1g| Protein 36.7g| Sodium 12mg

11.2.8 Pressure Canned Pinto Beans

Serves 6 jars | Prep Time: 25 minutes | Cook Time: 30 minutes

Ingredients

- Pinto beans - 2 lbs.
- Salt
- vinegar
- Water

Procedure:

1. Rinse and thoroughly wash your pinto beans. Overnight, immerse them in water.
2. Put the beans in a saucepan, cover with water by two inches, and bring to a boil over high heat. Bring the beans to a boil, then simmer for 30 minutes, stirring occasionally.
3. Clean jars should have a 1-inch headspace before being filled with beans. If you like, you may add a half tsp. of salt and vinegar to each pint jar.
4. Release the air bubbles before adding the cooking liquid to each jar. If required, add some of the cooking liquid.
5. To clean the jar rims, use a moist cloth. To tighten the rings, put the lids on the jars and

then fasten them. To can, place the jars in the pressure canner.

6. 75 minutes with 10 lbs. of pressure. After shutting off the heat, let the canner fully cool down before using it.

7. Remove the jars from the pressure canner and open them. Do not disrupt for the whole 24 hours. Retain the jars in a cold, dry location after removing the rings.

Nutrition per serving: Calories 245, fat 1g, carbs 30g Protein 15g, Sugars 0g, Fiber 15g| Sodium 407mg

11.2.9 Marinated Fava Beans

Serves: 2 | Prep Time: 15 minutes | Cook Time: 25 minutes

Ingredients

- fresh and minced garlic - 1 tsp.
- kosher salt - 1/2 tsp.
- ground black pepper - 1/4 tsp.
- fava beans – 1 1/2 lbs.
- fresh rosemary - 2 sprigs
- olive oil - 2 tbsps.
- red wine vinegar - 2 tbsps.
- water

Procedure:

1. Heat salted water in a pot. Remove the beans from their pods while the water is heating up. Meanwhile, add the beans and simmer until they are bright green and soft (approximately 3 minutes).

2. The beans should be drained and rinsed in cold water. Remove the fava beans from their shells and place them in a separate container.

3. In a mason jar, combine the vinegar, garlic, oil, rosemary, salt, and pepper.

4. Allow the canner to cool completely before using it again after turning off the heat.

5. Finally, fill the container with fava beans, seal it, and enjoy! Set your marinated beans in a refrigerator for a maximum of 3 days.

6. Before serving, soak the beans in the mixture for at least 15 minutes.

Nutrition per serving: Calories 195 Cal; Fat: 0 g; Carbs: 5 g; Protein 9 g

11.3 FRUIT

11.3.1 Apple Slices

Serves: 7 quarts | Prep Time: 25 mins | Cook Time: 5 mins

Ingredients:

- Apples - 19 lbs.
- Canning syrup - 1
- Water
- Lemon juice

Procedure:

1. Get a water bath canner ready.
2. Peel the apples and cut them into uniform slices (about 1/2 inch thick) to prepare them for canning.
3. To keep the peeled and sliced apple pieces from browning, set them in a bowl of cold water with a liberal splash of lemon juice (or dissolve 1/2 tsp. of ascorbic acid in 8 c. of cool water).
4. Bring your choice canning liquid to a boil in a kettle.
5. Drain any extra liquid from the apple slices by removing them from the water.
6. Carefully place the apple slices into the boiling canning liquid & simmer, stirring regularly, for 5 minutes, or until the apples are well cooked. To keep the apple pieces from falling apart, stir gently.
7. Fill the canning jars halfway with apples, leaving 1/2 inch headspace. Fill a 1/2-inch headspace with canning liquid and pour it over the apple pieces.
8. Before sealing the jars with 2 part canning lids, de-bubble the jars & make any final headspace adjustments.
9. For pints and quarts, process the jars in a water bath canner for almost 20 minutes. (The recipe is for a 7-quart canner batch at a lower height than 1000 feet; see comments for various batch sizes and altitudes.)
10. When the canning time is over, remove the jars and set them on the counter to cool. Check seals after 24 hours and keep any jars that aren't sealed in the refrigerator for quick use.
11. In the cupboard, sealed jars of carefully preserved apple slices will keep their optimal flavor for 12 to 18 months.

Nutrition per serving: Calories: 297 | Carbs 90g| Protein: 6g| Fat: 0g.

11.3.2 Mixed Fruit Cocktail

Serves: 6 pints | Prep Time: 10 mins | Cook Time: 1 hr.

Ingredients:

- Peaches - 3 lbs.
- Pears - 3 lbs.
- Seedless green grapes - 1 1/2 lbs.
- Maraschino cherries – 1 (10-oz.) jar
- Sugar - 3 c.
- Water - 4 c.
- Lemon juice

Procedure:

1. Remove the stems and wash the grapes before storing them in ascorbic acid or lemon juice. To soften the skins of ripe but hard peaches, place a couple at a time in boiling water for almost 1 to 1-1/2 mins. Skins should be dipped in cold water and then slipped off.
2. Half the grapes, remove the pits, cut them into 1/2-inch cubes, and retain them in the solution with the grapes. Pears should be peeled, halved, and cored. Cut into 1/2-inch cubes and combine with grapes & peaches in a solution.
3. Using a saucepan, add in water and sugar and allow to boil.
4. Drain the fruit mixture. To each heated jar, pour 1/2 c. of hot syrup. Then, leaving 1/2-inch headspace, add a few cherries and gradually fill the jar with the hot syrup and mixed fruit.
5. Do away with air bubbles and, adjust headspace if need be. Using a wet clean paper towel, wipe the jar rims.

78

6. Adjust the heated lids and bake for 20 minutes in a water bath.

Nutrition per serving: Calories: 269| Carbs 92g| Protein: 8g| Fat: 0.1g.

11.3.3 Pineapple Chunks

Serves: 6 half-pints | Prep Time: 15 mins | Cook Time: 15 mins

Ingredients:

- Raw Pineapples - 2
- Water - 2 c.
- Juice or Syrup - 2.5 c. per pineapple

Procedure:

1. Pineapple should be chopped into bits. For crushed pineapple, use large pieces, little chunks, or chopped pineapple. Select your preferred option.
2. Bring the pineapple to boiling in the canning liquid for 10 minutes to make a hot pack.
3. Fill your jars halfway with pineapple and juice/syrup, allowing a headspace of 1/2 inch.
4. Process 15 mins for half-pints and 20 mins for quarts in a water bath canner (adjusting for altitude).
5. Allow cooling to room temp after removing from the canner. Check jars for seals and use those that aren't sealed right away.

Nutrition per serving: Calories: 249| Carbs 159g| Protein: 5g| Fat: 0g.

11.3.4 Canning Grapefruit

Serves: 3-quart jars | Prep Time: 20 mins | Cook Time: 15 mins

Ingredients:

- Grapefruit - 7 ½ lbs.
- Syrup for Canning - 1 batch
- Water

Procedure:

1. Wash the grapefruit in cold water and drain it. Grapefruit should be peeled with a deep enough incision to remove the white pith and membrane. Remove the grapefruit pulp in one piece by cutting the membrane along each side

of one segment. Rep until all of the parts have been eliminated. Seeds should be discarded.
2. In a medium pot, make the Canning Syrup. Over medium-high heat, bring the mixture to a boil. Reduce to a low heat setting (180°F).
3. Fill a heated jar halfway with grapefruit, allowing a 12-inch headspace. Fill a 12-inch headspace with boiling syrup and pour it over the grapefruit. Air bubbles should be removed. Clean the rim of the jar. Adjust the band to fingertip-tightness and center the lid on the jar. In a boiling-water canner, place the jar on a rack placed over simmering water (180°F). Rep until all of the jars are full.
4. Place the rack in a pot of water that is just simmering. 1 inch of water must cover the jars. Increase the heat to medium-high, cover the canner, and bring the water to a boil. 10 minutes for pint or quart jars. Remove the top and turn off the heat. Allow 5 minutes for the jars to cool. Remove the jars from the canner, and do not retighten the bands if they are slack. Allow 12 hours for cooling. Seals for testing. Jars should be labeled and stored.
5. Grapefruit comes in a variety of flavors and sweetness levels. Choose the sugar syrup that best matches the grapefruit's sweetness.

Nutrition per serving: Calories: 349kcal| Carbs 82g| Protein: 2g| Fat: 0g.

11.3.5 Fresh Berries

Serves: 1 | Prep Time: 10 mins | Cook Time: 30 mins

Ingredients:

- Fresh berries – 1 gallon
- Lemon juice - 7 tbsps.
- Filtered water - 7 c.

Procedure:

1. Pour the following amount of lemon juice into jar: For each pint-sized jar, use 1 tablespoon; for each quart-sized jar, use 2 tablespoons.
2. Fill the container halfway with berries. Ensure the berries are clean, washed, and free of any leaves or stems before using them. Mushy or squishy berries should also be discarded.

3. Cover the jars halfway with water and leave a 12-inch gap at the top.
4. Place the lids on top. To seal and preserve the berries, use the water bath canning process (30 minutes for quart-sized jars or 15 minutes for pint-sized jars).

Nutrition

Calories: 768 | Carbs 71g | Protein: 22g | Fat: 49g.

11.3.6 Fresh Plums

Serves: 4 quart | Prep Time: 30 mins | Cook Time: 30 mins

Ingredients:

- Plums - 2 lbs. per quart jar
- Water
- Syrup or juice

Procedure:

1. Make sure you have a water bath canner ready.
2. Slice the plums in half and remove the pits for plum halves, or puncture the exterior with a toothpick for the whole plums with pits, to prepare them for canning.
3. Bring a canning liquid to a boil over high heat, either juice, water, or syrup.
4. Place the chopped fruit in the boiling liquid and simmer for 2 minutes for hot pack plums (recommended). Remove the saucepan from the heat and cover it with a lid. Allow the plums to slowly cook through in the heated liquid for 20-30 minutes. The heated fruit should then be packed into canning jars.
5. If you choose raw packing rather than hot packing, just put the prepped fruit into canning jars.
6. Pour the hot canning liquid over the plums for both hot and raw packing. This should fully cover them but allow 1/2 inch of headroom.
7. Remove the bubbles, adjust the headspace, and finger-tighten the lids using 2 part canning lids.
8. At altitudes below 1000 feet, the process in water bath canner for almost 20 mins (pints) or 25 minutes (quarts) in a water bath canner.
9. When the canning period is over, place the jars on a cloth on the counter to cool and check seals after 24 hours. Unsealed jars should be

kept in the refrigerator for immediate use, while sealed jars should be kept in the pantry.
10. Jars that have been properly treated and sealed should last 12-18 months on the pantry shelf.

Nutrition per serving: Calories: 249 | Carbs 16g | Protein: 2g | Fat: 0g.

11.3.7 Canning Guava Fruit

Serves: 2-pint jars | Prep Time: 15 mins | Cook Time: 15 mins

Ingredients:

- Guava fruit - 2 lbs. per quart
- Sugar - 2 c.
- Water - 5 c.

Procedure:

1. Begin by prepping the jars and boiling the water in the canner. When jars are ready to be processed, you want the canner to be hot but not boiling.
2. Remove the seeds from the guava fruit by washing, peeling, and halving it.
3. Bring the sugar syrup to a boil.
4. Remove the pan from the heat and add the guavas to the syrup.
5. Allow 30 minutes for the mixture to settle. This will slowly warm the apple all the way through.
6. Using a slotted spoon, remove the fruit from the syrup and pack it into heated jars.
7. Bring the syrup back to a boil, then cover the fruit with it, allowing 1/2" headroom.
8. Air bubbles should be removed. Place your seals and rings on the rims after wiping them clean.
9. In the heating canner, place the jars.
10. Adjust for altitude and process pints for 15 minutes or quarts for 20 minutes.

Nutrition per serving: Calories: 276 | Carbs 59g | Protein: 8g | Fat: 0.1g.

11.3.8 Canning Fresh Mango

Serves: 3 quarts | Prep Time: 15 mins | Cook Time: 15 mins

Ingredients:

- Mangoes, peeled & seeded - 9
- Sugar - 1/4 c.
- Water - 2 c.
- Lemon juice - 1

Procedure:

1. Peeled and seeded mangoes may be sliced into bits or left whole. Leave 1/2 inch headroom before packing the mango into mason jars.
2. To guarantee adequate acidity, add 1/4 c. lemon juice to each quart or 2 tbsp. of lemon juice to each pint. While you're making the canning syrup, set the jars aside.
3. On the burner, bring the sugar and water to a boil. To dissolve the sugar, stir it in.
4. In canning jars, pour the boiling syrup over the mangoes. Using a plastic tool, pop any air bubbles. 2 part lids are used to close the jars.
5. Use a water bath canner to finish the process. Pints and half-pints take 15 minutes to prepare, while quarts take 20 minutes.

Nutrition per serving: Calories: 249 | Carbs 11g | Protein: 2g | Fat: 0g.

11.3.9 Fresh Blueberries

Serves: 6 jars | Prep Time: 10 mins | Cook Time: 15 mins

Ingredients:

- Blueberries - 2.2 lbs.
- Water - 3 c.
- Granulated sugar - ½ c.
- Lemon juice - 3 tbsps.

Procedure:

1. Remove any damaged blueberries after washing them if you are using jars with a capacity of 350 ml/12 fl. Oz./ 12 cups, divide the berries between the jars, roughly 200 g/7 oz. berries into each jar. Fill the jars to the appropriate size, allowing around 2 cm/12-inch headspace if using smaller or bigger jars.
2. Fill a pot halfway with water and add lemon juice and sugar. Allow to come to a moderate boil, often stirring to ensure the sugar fully dissolves. Allow to bubble for one minute

before removing from the heat. Allow 5 minutes for cooling.

3. Drizzle the syrup over the blueberries, fully covering them. Clean the rims. The jars should be sealed and canned.
4. Fill a half-filled canner halfway with water. Allow the water to boil, then use a jar lifter to drop the jars into the water one at a time, or use the canner's canning rack to drop all the jars into the water at once. 2 12 to 5 cm/1 to 2 inches of water should cover the jars. If required, add extra boiling water.
5. Bring to a simmer, cover, and cook for 15 minutes, adding time if required to account for altitude. Allow sitting in the pot for 5 minutes.
6. Remove the jars using oven gloves and a jar lifter and cool thoroughly on folded kitchen towels or the cutting boards.

Nutrition per serving: Calories: 161 | Carbs 41g | Protein: 1g | Fat: 1g

11.3.10 Brandied Honey and Spice Pears

Serves: 6 pints | Prep Time: 35 minutes | Cook Time: 5 minutes

Ingredients:

- lemon juice - 1/2 c.
- whole cloves - 1/2 tbsp
- brandy - 1/4 c.
- honey – 1 1/2 c.
- crystallized ginger - 3 tbsps.
- apple juice, cranberry juice, or apple cider - 4 c.
- ripe and firm pears - 6 lb.
- cinnamon, break sticks into halves - 8 inches stick
- Ascorbic acid color keeper

Procedure:

1. Pears should be peeled and cut in half before being placed in the ascorbic acid to keep them from turning brown. Set away for a later time.
2. Preparation: Combine the apple juice with lemon juice, cloves, ginger and cinnamon in a 6-8 liter saucepan. Continue to whisk until the mixture is brought to a rolling boil. Lower the temperature.

3. Add the pear components to the syrup after draining. Add the brandy and raise the heat to bring the liquid to a boil. Simmer the pears for about five minutes, stirring regularly, at a low simmer.

4. Make sure to allow a half-inch headspace by using a slotted spoon to push the spears into the jars.

5. Maintain the half-inch headroom by ladling the syrup over the pears. Wipe the pint jar rims with a clean cloth and screw on the lids.

6. In a 10-lb. pressure canner, place the jars and process them under 10 lbs. of pressure.

7. Remove the lid from the canner and transfer the jars to a wire rack to cool. Allow them to cool for at least 24 hours before storing them in a cold, dry location.

Nutrition per serving: Calories 262, fat 0g, carbs 61g Protein 1g, Sugars 55g, Fiber 6g| Sodium 5 mg, Potassium 253mg

11.3.11   Pressure Canned Honey-Lavender Peaches

Serves: 12 pints | Prep Time: 60 minutes | Cook Time: 5 minutes

Ingredients:

- lemon - 1
- dried lavender buds - 1 tbsp
- salt - 1/2 tbsp
- honey – 1 3/4 c.
- ripe peaches - 15 lbs.
- Riesling - 2/3 c.
- water - 4 c.

Procedure:

1. A big kettle of water should be brought to a rolling boil. Cook the peaches for 30-60 seconds, or until the skin begins to peel, in a pot of hot water, in batches.

2. Transfer the pitches from the hot water to a large basin of ice-cold water using a slotted spoon.

3. Peel the peaches after rinsing them in cool water.

4. Discard the pits by slicing them in half lengthwise. Using a large pot, combine 4 c. of water with 4 tbsps. of honey, 2 tbsps. of Riesling, and a pinch of salt. In a medium-sized saucepan, combine the honey, lavender, water, and salt and bring to a boil.

5. Using a vegetable peeler, cut three-inch strips of lemon peel. Lemons may be saved for various use.

6. The sliced side of the peaches should face down in jars. Set the syrup into the jars, then add the lemon peel and leave a 1/2-inch headspace between the jars.

7. Wipe the rims of the jars with a damp cloth before putting on the lids and rings. Wipe the jar rims clean before adding the lids and rings. In a pressure canner, bring the temperature to 10 lbs. of pressure and process the jars for 70 minutes.

8. Before taking the jars from the canner and setting them on a cooling rack, let the canner cool down.

Nutrition per serving: Calories 77, fat 0g, carbs 17g Protein 1g, Sugars 18g, Fiber 2g| Sodium 22mg, Potassium 213mg

11.3.12   Canned Green Tea Chai-Spiced Peaches

Serves: 12 pints | Prep Time: 60 minutes | Cook Time: 5 minutes

Ingredients:

- loose green tea leaves - 1 tbsp
- packed brown sugar - 1/2 c.
- black peppercorns - 10
- garlic cloves - 10
- green cardamom pods - 10
- granulated sugar– 1 1/3 c.
- ripe peaches - 15 lbs.
- fresh ginger, peeled and thinly sliced - 3-inch piece
- cinnamon – 3 inches sticks
- water – 4 1/2 c.

Procedure:

1. A big kettle of water should be brought to a rolling boil. Cook the peaches for 30-60 seconds, or until the skin begins to peel, in a pot of hot water, in batches.

2. Transfer the pitches from the hot water to a large basin of ice-cold water using a slotted spoon.
3. Peel the peaches after rinsing them in cool water.
4. Discard the pits by slicing them in half lengthwise.
5. Cook the spices in a Dutch oven with 4 and a half c. of water. Add the sugars and spices. Stir until well-combined.
6. Cook, stirring constantly until the sugar is completely dissolved. Turn heat down and simmer for 20 minutes after bringing to a boil.
7. After the heat has been turned off, add the green tea leaves and combine well. Give it a five-minute break and then reopen. Strain the syrup using a sieve. Throw away the solids.
8. Fill the sterilized jars with peaches and syrup, allowing about a half-inch headspace in each.
9. Place lids and rings on jars and wipe the rims. When processed under 10 lbs. of pressure, the jars need 60 minutes to complete their journey from start to finish.
10. Remove the jars from the canner after it has cooled down. Store them when they've cooled completely on a wire rack.

Nutrition per serving: Calories 69, fat 0g, carbs 15g Protein 1g, Sugars 16g, Fiber 2g | Sodium 1mg, Potassium 189mg

11.3.13   Canned Strawberries

Serve: 4 | Prep Time: 10 minutes | Cook Time: 20 minutes

Ingredients:

- strawberries, washed & hulled - 4 c.
- citric acid - ¼ tsp
- sugar - ½ c.

Procedure:

1. Add strawberries and sugar in a large pot, cover, and let sit for 6 hours.
2. Add citric acid and place pot on heat and cook for 1 minute or until strawberries are heated through.
3. Remove pot from heat. Pack strawberries into the clean jars and top with the strawberry juice

liquid. Leave 1/2 –inch headspace. Remove air bubbles.
4. Seal jars with lids and process for 10 minutes in a boiling water bath.
5. Remove jars from water bath and let it cool completely.
6. Check seals of jars. Label and store.

Nutrition per serving: Calories 140, Fat 0.4 g, Carbs 36.1 g, Sugar 32.1 g, Protein 1 g, Cholesterol 0 mg

11.3.14   Canned Pineapple

Serve: 24 | Prep Time: 10 minutes | Cook Time: 60 minutes

Ingredients:

- pineapples, peeled, cored & cut into chunks - 6
- water - 5 c.
- sugar - 1 c.

Procedure:

1. Add sugar and water into the pot and bring to boil, stir constantly until sugar is dissolved. Reduce heat to low.
2. Add pineapples chunks and cook for 10 minutes.
3. Pack pineapple chunks into the clean jars. Leave ½-inch headspace.
4. Pour hot sugar syrup over pineapple chunks. Leave a headspace of ½-inch. Do away with air bubbles.
5. Seal jars with lids and process in a boiling water bath for 10 minutes.
6. Remove jars from the water bath and let it cool completely.
7. Check seals of jars. Label and store.

Nutrition per serving: Calories 72, Fat 0.1 g, Carbs 19.2 g, Sugar 16.5 g, Protein 0.4 g, Cholesterol 0 mg

11.3.15   Canned Oranges

Serve: 6 | Prep Time: 10 minutes | Cook Time: 15 minutes

Ingredients:

- oranges, peel, remove white pith & divide into segments - 3
- whole cloves - 5
- water - 2 c.

- cinnamon - ½ tsp
- sugar - 1 c.

Procedure:

1. using a saucepan, add sugar and water. Add in cinnamon and stir. Allow to boil.
2. Reduce heat intensity and simmer for 5 minutes.
3. Pack orange segments into the clean jars and top with cloves.
4. Pour hot sugar syrup over orange. Leave a headspace of ¼-inch. Do away with air bubbles.
5. Seal jars with lids and process in a boiling water bath for 10 minutes.
6. Remove jars from the water bath and let it cool completely.
7. Check seals of jars. Label and store.

Nutrition per serving: Calories 169, Fat 0.1 g, Carbs 44.3 g, Sugar 41.9 g, Protein 0.9 g, Cholesterol 0 mg

11.3.16   Canned Pears

Serve: 7 | Prep Time: 10 minutes | Cook Time: 25 minutes

Ingredients:

- pears, peel & slice - 18 lbs.
- water - 6 c.
- sugar - 1 c.

Procedure:

1. Add water and sugar in a saucepan and bring to boil over medium heat.
2. Once sugar syrup starts boiling, reduce the heat intensity to low.
3. Add pears and into the sugar syrup and simmer for 5 minutes.
4. Pack pears into the clean jars. Leave ¼-inch headspace.
5. Pour hot sugar syrup over pears. Leave ¼-inch headspace. Remove air bubbles.
6. Seal jars with lids and process for 20 minutes in a boiling water bath.
7. Remove jars from water bath and allow to cool completely.
8. Check seals of jars. Label and store.

Nutrition per serving: Calories 784, Fat 1.7 g, Carbs 206.5 g, Sugar 142.5 g, Protein 4.3 g, Cholesterol 0 mg

11.3.17   Canned Peaches

Serve: 8 | Prep Time: 10 minutes | Cook Time: 30 minutes

Ingredients:

- peaches - 4 lbs
- water - 8 c.
- sugar - 1 ½ c.

Procedure:

1. Add peaches into the boiling water and cook for 3 minutes.
2. Remove peaches from boiling water and place into the bowl of ice water.
3. Peel peaches discard the pit and cut into slices.
4. Pack peaches into the clean jars. Leave ¼-inch headspace.
5. Add water and sugar in a saucepan and bring to boil, stir until sugar is dissolved.
6. Pour hot sugar syrup over pears. Leave a headspace of ¼-inch. Remove air bubbles.
7. Seal jars with lids and process in a boiling water bath for 20 minutes.
8. Remove jars from the water bath and let it cool completely.
9. Check seals of jars. Label and store.

Nutrition per serving: Calories 170, Fat 0.2 g, Carbs 44.5 g, Sugar 44.5 g, Protein 0.7 g, Cholesterol 0 mg

11.3.18   Canned Mango

Serve: 6 | Prep Time: 10 minutes | Cook Time: 30 minutes

Ingredients:

- peeled mangoes, seeded & cut into chunks - 8
- sugar - 4 tbsps.
- fresh lemon juice - 3 tbsps
- Water

Procedure:

1. Pack mango into the jars. Leave ½-inch headspace.
2. Add 1 tbsp. of lemon juice to each jar.

3. Using a pot, add 2 cups of water and sugar and allow to boil. Stir well to ensure the sugar dissolves.
4. Pour hot sugar syrup over the mangoes.
5. Seal jar with lids. Process in a water bath canner for 15 minutes.
6. Remove jars from the water bath and let it cool completely.
7. Check seals of jars. Label and store.

Nutrition per serving: Calories 300, Fat 2 g, Carbs 75 g, Sugar 70 g, Protein 3 g, Cholesterol 0 mg

11.3.19   Canned Apricots

Serve: 8 | Prep Time: 10 minutes | Cook Time: 20 minutes

Ingredients:

- apricots, wash, cut in half and remove the stone - 2 lbs
- water - 4 c.
- sugar - 2 c.

Procedure:

1. Add water and sugar in a pot and cook over medium heat until sugar is melted.
2. Add apricots into the jars.
3. Pour sugar syrup over apricots.
4. Cover jars with lids.
5. Place jars in a large pot and cover them with water. Bring to the boil and simmer for 30 minutes.
6. Turn off the heat and let the jars cool completely.
7. Check seals of jars. Label and store.

Nutrition per serving: Calories 240, Fat 1 g, Carbs 62 g, Sugar 60 g, Protein 1.5 g, Cholesterol 0 mg

11.3.20   Canned Cherries

Serve: 4 | Prep Time: 10 minutes | Cook Time: 15 minutes

Ingredients:

- cherries, pitted - 2 c.
- whole allspice - 4
- cinnamon stick - 1
- vanilla extract - 1 tsp

- lemon juice - 1 tbsp
- water - 1 c.
- sugar - 1 c.

Procedure:

1. Using a saucepan, add in sugar and water and allow to boil, stir well to dissolve the sugar.
2. Remove saucepan from heat and allow to cool.
3. Add vanilla extract and lemon juice and stir well.
4. Add allspice and cinnamon into each jar then add cherries. Leave 3/4–inch headspace.
5. Pour sugar syrup over cherries. Leave ½-inch headspace.
6. Seal jar with lid and store in the refrigerator.

Nutrition per serving: Calories 230, Fat 0.3 g, Carbs 59.7 g, Sugar 56.7 g, Protein 0.8 g, Cholesterol 0 mg

11.3.21   Canned Blueberries

Serve: 4 | Prep Time: 10 minutes | Cook Time: 20 minutes

Ingredients:

- blueberries, rinsed - 3 lbs
- Water - 4 c.
- sugar - 1 c.

Procedure:

1. Add water and sugar in a saucepan and bring to boil, stir until sugar is dissolved.
2. Pack blueberries in clean jars then pour hot sugar syrup over blueberries. Leave 1/2-inch headspace.
3. Seal jars with lids and process for 20 minutes in a boiling water bath.
4. Remove jars from water bath and allow it cool completely.
5. Check seals of jars. Label and store.

Nutrition per serving: Calories 382, Fat 1.2 g, Carbs 99.3 g, Sugar 83.8 g, Protein 2.6 g, Cholesterol 0 mg

11.4 BUTTERS

11.4.1 Lavender Apricot Butter

Serves: 2-pint jars | Prep Time: 5 minutes | Cook Time: 45 minutes

Ingredients:

- peeled apricots, chopped, and pitted - 25
- freshly squeezed lemon juice - 3 tbsps.
- lavender buds (food grade) - 2 ½ tbsps.
- white sugar - 3 c.
- water - 1/2 c.

Procedure:

1. Tightly wrap the lavender buds in a cheesecloth. Add the water and apricots to a large pot and place over medium to high heat.
2. Add in the wrapped lavender buds and bring to a boil. Simmer and let cook until the apricots become soft and the lavender flavor is to your liking.
3. Remove and use your immersion blender to blend the apricots to desired texture. Mix the sugar and lemon juice and return to heat until it starts boiling gently.
4. Lower the heat and continue stirring to ensure it doesn't burn. Turn off the heat when the butter starts sticking to the spoon.
5. Prepare a hot water bath, scoop the fruit butter into the prepared jars, and seal tightly. Process for 15 minutes, then let it cool before storing.

Nutrition per serving: Calories: 96; Fat: 0 g; Carbs: 26 g; Protein: 0 g

11.4.2 Cinnamon Apple Butter

Serves: 2-pint jars | Prep Time: 5 minutes | Cook Time: 7 hours

Ingredients:

- chopped Granny Smith apples - 10 c.
- raw honey - 1/2 c.
- dark brown sugar - 1/3 c.
- allspice - ½ tsp
- ground cloves - ½ tsp

Procedure:

1. Combine the spices, honey, and sugar in your slow cooker until well mixed, then toss in the chopped apples and stir well until evenly coated.
2. Cook on low for 6 hours 30 minutes until the apple is super soft and breaks apart. Remove the lid and cook within 30 more minutes, so the butter becomes thick.
3. Scoop the butter into storage jars, tightly seal and process in a water bath for 10 minutes. Let it cool before storing.

Nutrition per serving: Calories: 84; Protein: 0 g Carbs: 22 g; Fat: 0 g

11.4.3 Plum Butter

Serves: 2-pint jars | Prep Time: 10 minutes | Cook Time: 80 minutes

Ingredients:

- plums, chopped and pitted - 8 c.
- mandarins, zested, peeled, and chopped - 2
- raw honey - ¼ c.
- ground cinnamon - 1 tsp
- ground allspice - 1/2 tsp
- pure vanilla extract - 1 tsp

Procedure:

1. Puree the plums in your blender or food processor, then pass through a strainer to remove the skins. Transfer the puree to your heavy-bottomed pan.
2. Squeeze the juice of the mandarins in the pan and add the zest and the remaining ingredients.
3. Place your pan over medium to high heat and bring to a boil, then lower the heat and simmer for about 1 hour and 20 minutes, removing the zest after 20 minutes of cooking, stirring so it doesn't stick.
4. Scoop into mason jars, cover tightly, and process in a water bath for 10 minutes. Let it cool before storing.

Nutrition per serving: Calories: 16; Fat: 0 g; Carbs: 4 g; Protein: 0 g

11.4.4 Vanilla Pear Butter

Serves: 4-pint jars | Prep Time: 5 minutes | Cook Time: 0 minutes

Ingredients:

- pears, chopped - 10 c.
- fresh lemon juice - ¼ c.
- orange juice - ¼ c.
- lemon zest - 1 tsp
- orange zest - 1 tbsp
- water, more if needed - ½ c.
- sugar - 2 c.
- cardamom - ¾ tsp
- vanilla bean paste - 2 tsps
- nutmeg - ¾ tsp
- cinnamon - 1 tsp

Procedure:

1. Combine the chopped pears, lemon zest and juice, orange zest, and water in a large pot and bring to a gentle boil.
2. Lower the heat and simmer within 20 minutes while stirring to ensure it doesn't stick to the bottom.
3. Blend the cooked pears until achieving desired consistency, then transfer the puree to a saucepan. Stir in the sugar, vanilla paste, orange juice, and spices.
4. Continue to stir until the sugar dissolves over medium heat and the utter thickens. It should stick to a spoon. Ladle the batter into prepared storage jars, leaving a ¼ inch headspace.
5. Tightly seal the jars and process for canning by dipping them in a hot water bath for 15 minutes. Let it cool before storing.

Nutrition per serving: Calories: 33; Carbs: 6.3 g; Fat: 0 g; Protein: 0 g

11.4.5 Pumpkin Butter

Serving Size: 2 jars | Prep Time: 15 minutes | Cook Time: 20 minutes

Ingredients:

- dry pectin – 1 (2 oz.) package
- solidly packed pumpkin puree - 1 (29 oz.) can
- pumpkin pie spice - 1 tbsp.
- white sugar - 4 1/2 c.

Direction:

1. Pumpkin puree, dry pectin, and pumpkin pie spice should be heated in a medium saucepan over high heat, along with the solid pack. Boil the mixture for a few minutes. Add the sugar all at once and stir until it is completely dissolved.
2. Stir the mixture often until it reaches a full boil and then removes it from the heat. For a minute, bring the mixture to a boil. Pour it into the sterilized containers as soon as you remove it from the heat.
3. Keep the containers in the refrigerator until ready for serving.

Nutrition per serving: Calories 59 | Protein: 0.1g, Carbs: 15.1g | Fat: 0g Sodium: 31mg

11.4.6 Apple Cranberry Butter

Serves: 12 | Prep Time: 15 minutes | Cook Time: 1 hour

Ingredients:

- fresh cranberries - 2 lbs.
- maple syrup - 1 ½ c.
- lemon juice - 2 tbsps.
- water - 1 c.
- apples, cored and chopped - 2 lbs.

Procedure:

1. In a saucepan, combine apples, cranberries, water, and lemon juice. Over medium heat, bring the mixture to a boil and cook for a few minutes until apples are tender.
2. Smoothly puree the apple mixture. Put the pureed mixture back in the pan and heat it again. Cook the ingredients for a few minutes after adding the maple syrup until it has thickened.
3. When the apple cranberry butter is ready, remove it from the heat and spoon it into the prepared jars. Using lids, secure the jars. To

can, use a water bath canner for 20 minutes of processing time.

4. Remove jars from water bath and let them cool completely. Make sure the seals on jars are intact. Then, label and store.

Nutrition per serving: Calories 164| Fat 0.3 g| Carbs 38.5 g, Sugar 30.1 g| Protein 0.1 g, Cholesterol 0 mg

11.4.7 Apple Butter

Serves: 14 | Prep Time: 30 minutes | Cook Time: 25 minutes

Ingredients:

- water - ½ c.
- ground nutmeg - ½ tsp
- ground allspice - 1 ½ tsp
- maple syrup - 1 c.
- ground cloves - 1 tsp
- apples, cored and quartered - 10 lbs.
- apple juice - 2 c.
- lemon juice - 3 tbsps.
- ground cinnamon - 3 tsps.

Procedure:

1. In a large stockpot, combine the apples, water, and lemon juice. Simmer over medium-high heat with a lid on.
2. Cook the apples for approximately 20 minutes until they are tender. Make a smooth puree out of the apple combination.
3. Add the apple purée to a slow cooker and simmer for a few hours. Make a well-combined mixture of apple juice, maple syrup, and seasonings.
4. To get a thick consistency, set the slow cooker to high and simmer for a few minutes.
5. Pour the apple butter into the clean jars in this order: Using lids, secure the jars.
6. For the next fifteen minutes, put all of the above into a water bath canner and seal it.
7. Set aside to cool to room temperature when you have removed the jars from the water bath. Make sure the seals on jars are intact. Then, label and store.

Nutrition per serving: Calories 161| Protein 0.5 g Carbs 41.8 g| Fat 0.5 g, Sugar 33.5 g

11.4.8 Banana Butter

Serves: 2 jars | Prep Time: 15 minutes | Cook Time: 20 minutes

Ingredients:

- pure vanilla extract - 1 tbsp.
- dark brown sugar - 1/2 c.
- cinnamon - 1/4 tsp.
- ripe bananas, sliced - 10
- bourbon - 2 tbsps.

Procedure:

1. Puree the bananas and sugar in a blender or food processor until they are completely smooth. Add the bourbon to a heavy-bottomed skillet and allow to boil over medium-high source of heat.
2. To thicken, allow to boil mildly and whisk regularly, then reduce the heat to a simmer. Remove the pan from the heat and mix in the cinnamon and vanilla. Scoop into jars, seal, and store in the refrigerator.

Nutrition per serving: Calories 102, Fat 0.3 g| Sodium 2 mg, Carbs 24.5g| Protein 0.9 g

11.4.9 Rhubarb Butter

Serves: 8 | Prep Time: 20 minutes | Cook Time: 50 minutes

Ingredients:

- rhubarb, chopped - 1 ½ lb.
- cinnamon - 11/2 tsp
- vanilla - 2 ½ tsps.
- brown sugar - 2 ¾ c.
- water - 2 c.

Direction:

1. Start by putting all of the ingredients into a saucepan and setting the heat to medium-low.
2. Simmer for 45 minutes on low heat. Turn on your food processor and blend until it's smooth.
3. Rinse and dry the jars, then fill them with rhubarb butter and seal. Using lids, secure the jars. Ten minutes in a water bath canner.

4. Wait until they are at room temperature before removing them from the heat source. fully.
5. Inspect the jar seals. Then, label and store.

Nutrition per serving: Calories 215| Protein 0.8 g| Carbs 54.1 g| Fat 0.3 g, Sugar 49.4 g

11.4.10   Tropical Fruit Butter

Serves: 2 Jars | Prep Time: 10 Minutes | Cook Time: 30 Minutes

Ingredients

- crushed pineapple, don't discard the juice - 1 can
- large ripe bananas, thinly sliced - 5
- fresh coconut, chopped - ¼ c.
- freshly squeezed lemon juice - ¼ c.
- brown sugar - 1 ½ c.

Procedure:

1. Using a heavy-bottomed saucepan, bring the ingredients to a boil over medium to high heat. Cook, stirring occasionally, for 20-30 minutes or until the fruit is tender.
2. Scoop out the necessary amount of thick butter into storage jars and process to desired smoothness.
3. Refrigerate or process for canning when a tight seal has been achieved.

Nutrition per serving: Calories: 41; Protein: 0 g; Carbs: 5.7 g; Fat: 0 g; fiber: 3.1 g; Sodium: 3 mg

11.4.11   Peach Butter

Serves: 2 Jars | Prep Time: 10 Minutes | Cook Time: 30 Minutes

Ingredients

- pure vanilla extract - ½ tsp.
- ground cinnamon - ½ tsp.
- brown sugar or adjust to taste - ¼ c.
- freshly squeezed lemon juice - 1 tsp.
- peeled peaches, pitted & chopped - 6 c.

Procedure

1. Using a large saucepan over medium intensity heat, combine all the ingredients mentioned, stirring constantly so that nothing sticks to the bottom.
2. Puree the peaches in a blender until they reach the appropriate butter consistency after simmering for 30 minutes.
3. Once chilled, transfer to Mason jars, seal, and store in the refrigerator.

Nutrition per serving: Calories: 36; Protein: 0 g; Carbs: 3.1 g; Fat: 0 g; Fiber: 1.9 g; Sodium: 1.1mg

11.4.12   Apple Pear Butter

Serve: 6 | Prep Time: 10 minutes | Cook Time: 1 hour 30 minutes

Ingredients:

- ripe pears, cored & diced - 4
- vanilla - 1 tsp
- lemon juice - ½
- nutmeg - ¼ tsp
- cinnamon - 1 ½ tsp
- brown sugar - 3 tbsps.
- maple syrup - ½ c.
- apple cider vinegar - 1 ½ c.
- apples, peel, cored & diced - 2
- salt - Pinch

Procedure:

1. Using a blender, set in all the above ingredients and blend well to obtain a smooth consistency.
2. Pour blended puree into the saucepan and allow to boil over medium-high source of heat. Reduce heat intensity and simmer for 30 minutes.
3. Stir well and continue simmering for 1 ½ hour.
4. Remove pan from heat and let it cool completely.
5. Pour apple butter in a clean jar. Seal jar with lid and store in the refrigerator.

Nutrition per serving: Calories 221, Fat 0.4 g, Carbs 54.7 g, Sugar 41.7 g, Protein 0.7 g, Cholesterol 0 mg

11.4.13   Cranberry Butter

Serves: 4 | Prep Time: 10 minutes | Cook Time: 4 hours

Ingredients:

- cranberries, rinsed - 24 oz
- apple cider - 1 c.
- cinnamon stick - 1
- brown sugar - 1 c.

Procedure:

1. Add all ingredients into the crockpot and stir well.
2. Cover and cook on high for 2 hours.
3. Remove cinnamon stick and puree the cranberry mixture in the food processer.

4. Strain cranberry mixture through a mesh strainer.
5. Return cranberry puree into your crockpot and cook on high for 2 hours more.
6. Pour cranberry butter in a clean jar. Leave a headspace of ½-inch. Remove air bubbles.
7. Seal jars with lids and process in a boiling water bath for 10 minutes.
8. Remove jars from the water bath and let it cool completely.
9. Check seals of jars. Label and store.

Nutrition per serving: Calories 260, Fat 0.1 g, Carbs 58 g, Sugar 48 g, Protein 0.1 g, Cholesterol 0 mg

11.4.14   Spiced Pear Butter

Servse: 8 | Prep Time: 10 minutes | Cook Time: 40 minutes

Ingredients:

- pears, peel & dice - 5
- nutmeg - ¼ tsp
- ginger, minced - ½ tsp
- cinnamon - 1 tsp
- brown sugar - 1 tbsp
- maple syrup - 2 tbsps.
- lemon juice - 2 tsps.
- salt - 1/8 tsp.

Procedure:

1. Using a saucepan, add in all the above ingredients and set over medium-high source of heat. Allow to boil
2. Reduce the heat intensity to medium-low and simmer for about 30 minutes.
3. Using immersion blender puree the pear mixture until smooth and simmer for 10 minutes more.
4. Remove pan from heat and allow to cool completely.
5. Pour pear butter in a clean jar. Seal jar with lid and store in the refrigerator.

Nutrition per serving: Calories 95, Fat 0.2 g, Carbs 24.7 g, Sugar 16.9 g, Protein 0.5 g, Cholesterol 0 mg

11.4.15   Mango Peach Butter

Serves: 8 | Prep Time: 10 minutes | Cook Time: 5 hours 30 minutes

Ingredients:

- peaches, peeled & quartered - 3 lbs
- water - ½ c.

- lemon juice - 1
- sugar - 1 c.

Procedure:

1. Using a crockpot, add in all ingredients and cook on low settings for 2 ½ hours.
2. Stir everything well and cook for 2-3 hours more or until fruit mixture is softened.
3. Using immersion blender puree the fruit mixture until smooth.
4. Pour fruit butter in a clean jar. Seal jar with lid and store in the refrigerator.

Nutrition per serving: Calories 116, Fat 0.2 g, Carbs 30.3 g, Sugar 30.3 g, Protein 0.5 g, Cholesterol 0 mg

11.4.16   Blueberry Butter

Serve: 16 | Prep Time: 10 minutes | Cook Time: 6 hours

Ingredients:

- fresh blueberries - 5 c.
- ground cinnamon - 1 tsp
- lemon juice - 1
- sugar - 1 c.

Procedure:

1. Using a blender, add blueberries and blend to obtain a smooth consistency.
2. In a crockpot, add blended blueberries and remaining ingredients and stir.
3. Cook for 1 hour on low while covered.
4. Remove crockpot lid and cook on low for 4-5 hours until thickened. Stir frequently.
5. Ladle blueberry butter into the clean jars.
6. Seal jar with lid and store in a cool and dry place.

Nutrition per serving: Calories 72, Fat 0.3 g, Carbs 20 g, Sugar 16 g, Protein 0.5 g, Cholesterol 0 mg

11.5 STEW, SOUPS AND BROTHS

11.5.1 Mexican Beef Garden Soup

Serves: 9 one-quart jars | Prep Time: 20 minutes | Cook time: 50 minutes

Ingredients:

- beef chuck roast, cubed - 5 lbs.
- corn - 2 c.
- black pepper - 1 tbsp.
- carrots, cut into rounds - 2
- peeled sweet potatoes, chopped - 2
- oil - 2 tbsps.
- poblano chili peppers, chopped without seeds - 4
- beef broth - 5 quarts
- Roma tomatoes, chopped without seeds - 8
- chopped onions - 1 ½ c.
- jalapeño peppers, chopped without seeds - 4
- cloves garlic, minced - 12
- salt - 2 tbsps.
- chili powder - 1 tbsp.

Procedure:

1. Brown beef in the hot oil, do it in batches if needed. Add broth, let it boil, turn the heat low and allow to simmer for 75 minutes.
2. Add the rest of the ingredients. Boil for 5 minutes.
3. In sterilized hot jars, add the mixture, leave half-inch space from above. Remove any air bubbles. You should wipe the rim of the jar, place the lid to the top and screw the bands (do not screw too tightly).
4. Process the jars in the pressure canner at 10 lbs. (weight) or 11 lbs. (dial) for 75 minutes. Make sure to adjust for altitude. Completely drop the pressure to zero; wait for 10 minutes.
5. Take the jars out and cool for 12 to 24 hours, and the lid should not pop down or up. Store in a cool, dark place

Nutrition per serving: Calories 260 Protein 32 g Carbs 16 g

11.5.2 Beef Stew with Vegetables

Serves: 14 pints | Prep Time: 20 minutes | Cook time: 30 minutes

Ingredients:

- vegetable oil - 1 tbsp.
- salt - 4 tsps.
- stew beef - 5 lbs.
- peeled potatoes, cubed - 12 c.
- sliced carrots - 8 c.
- pepper - ½ tsp.
- chopped celery - 3 c.
- onions – 3 c.
- thyme - 1 tsp.

Procedure:

1. Brown meat in hot oil. Add the vegetables & seasoning, add water.
2. Let it come to a boil for a few minutes.
3. In sterilized hot jars, add the mixture, leave half-inch space from above. Remove any air bubbles. You should wipe the rim of the jar, place the lid to the top and screw the bands (do not screw too tightly).
4. Process the jars in the pressure canner at 10 lbs. (weight) or 11 lbs. (dial) for 75 minutes. Make sure to adjust for altitude. Completely drop the pressure to zero; wait for 10 minutes.
5. Take the jars out and cool for 12 to 24 hours, and the lid should not pop down or up. Store in a cool, dark place.

Nutrition per serving: Calories 301 Protein 23.8 g Carbs 10 g

11.5.3 Spicy Roasted Pork Broth

Serves: 6-pint jars | Prep Time: 15 minutes | Cook Time: 35 minutes

Ingredients:

- pork shoulder, boneless, trimmed & cut into 1½-inch cubes - 3 lb.
- salt - 4 tsps.

- ground black pepper - ½ tsp
- canola oil - 1 tbsp
- chicken bone broth - 2-quart
- onion, halved vertically and cut crosswise into thin slices - 1 (8-oz)
- red pepper, dried, crushed - 2 tbsps.
- dried oregano - 1½ tbsps.
- garlic cloves, minced - 3

Procedure:

1. Preheat your oven to attain 428 F.
2. Place pork and sprinkle black pepper and 1 tsp salt on an aluminum foil rimmed baking sheet.
3. Drizzle with oil and toss. Arrange in a single layer and bake within 30 minutes or until the pork turns brown.
4. Meanwhile, take a 4-quart stainless-steel Dutch oven or skillet, and add broth, salt, onion, pepper, oregano, and garlic. Let it boil, reduce flame, cover, and simmer for 5 minutes.
5. Transfer the broth to hot jars with pork cubes. Leave headspace of 1-inch. Clean the rim of the glass jar. Place the lid and apply a band around it. Adjust to ensure that the lid is tight.
6. Place jars on racks with simmering 2-inches water to 180 F in a pressure canner.
7. Place lid on canner, adjust medium-high heat. Vent steam for 10 minutes at 11 lbs. pressure (dial gauge) or 10 lbs. (weighted-gauge) canner.
8. The next step is processing the jars for about 1 hour and 15 minutes. Turn off the canner, and remove the lid after two minutes when pressure turns zero. Keep the jars in the canner for 10 minutes more.

Nutrition per serving: Calories: 50 | Carbs: 2g | Fat: 0g | Protein: 10g

11.5.4 Chicken & Corn Soup

Serves: 16 pints | Prep Time: 20 minutes | Cook time: 30 minutes

Ingredients:

- Salt – ¼ tsp.
- Pepper – ¼ tsp.
- corn kernels - 8 c.
- shredded cooked chicken - 6 c.
- diced onion - 2 c.

- chicken stock - 32 c.

Procedure:

1. In a pan, add stock (2 cups) with onion & kernels. Let it come to a boil, turn the heat low and simmer for 5 minutes.
2. Add all ingredients to a pan, simmer for 5 minutes.
3. In sterilized hot jars, add the mixture, leave half-inch space from above. Remove any air bubbles. Ensure you wipe the rim of your jar, place set lid on the top and screw the bands (do not screw too tightly).
4. Process the jars in the pressure canner at 10 lbs. (weight) or 11 lbs. (dial) for 75 minutes. Make sure to adjust for altitude. Completely drop the pressure to zero; wait for 10 minutes.
5. Take the jars out and cool for 12 to 24 hours, and the lid should not pop down or up. Store in a cool, dark place

Nutrition per serving: Calories 309 Protein 21 g Carbs 11 g

11.5.5 Carrot-Fennel Soup

Serves: 12 pints | Prep Time: 20 minutes | Cook time: 50 minutes

Ingredients:

- fennel, thinly sliced - 2 bulbs
- vegetable stock - 6 c.
- Water – 6 c.
- olive oil - 1 tbsp.
- Salt – ¼ tsp.
- carrots, sliced - 4 lbs.
- white pepper - ½ tsp.
- water

Procedure:

1. In oil, sauté the fennel until translucent.
2. Add carrots and stock to the fennel. Let it come to a boil, turn the heat low and simmer until carrot is tender.
3. Puree with a stick blender, add water with salt & pepper.
4. Simmer for half an hour.
5. In sterilized hot jars, add the mixture, leave half-inch space from above. Remove any air

bubbles. Ensure you wipe the rim of the jar, place the lid on top and screw the bands (do not screw too tightly).

6. Process the jars in the pressure canner at 10 lbs. (weight) or 11 lbs. (dial) for 40 minutes. Make sure to adjust for altitude. Completely drop the pressure to zero; wait for 10 minutes.

7. Take the jars out and cool for 12 to 24 hours, and the lid should not pop down or up. Store in a cool, dark place.

Nutrition per serving: Calories 209 Protein 10.5 g Carbs 7 g

11.5.6 French Onion Soup

Serves: 8-pint jars | Prep Time: 15 minutes | Cook Time: 1 hour & 17 minutes

Ingredients:

- butter - 1 tbsp.
- onions, thinly sliced - 4 lb.
- salt - 1 tbsp.
- ground black pepper - 1 tsp.
- dried thyme - 1 tsp.
- dry white wine - 3 c.
- beef, chicken, or vegetable broth - 3-quart

Procedure:

1. Melt butter on medium-low heat in an 8-quart Stainless-steel Dutch oven or skillet. Add onion, broth, salt, pepper, thyme, and 2 c. of wine.

2. Cover it and cook for 60 minutes or more until the onion becomes tender with frequent stirring.

3. Uncover, and cook until onion turns caramel color. Add 1 c. of wine, cook for 2 minutes, stir, and bring it to a boil. Reduce flame and let it simmer uncovered for 15 minutes.

4. In hot jars, transfer the hot soup and leave a headspace of 1-inch. Do away with air bubbles. Ensure you clean rim of glass jar. Place the lid and apply a band around it. Adjust to ensure that the lid is tight.

5. Place jars on racks with simmering water to 180 F in a pressure canner.

6. Place lid on canner, adjust medium-high heat. Vent steam for 10 minutes at 10 lbs. for the weighted-gauge canner or 11 lbs. pressure for the dial gauge.

7. Process the pint jars for 60 minutes, turn off the canner, and remove the lid after two minutes when pressure turns zero. Keep the jars in the canner for 10 minutes more.

8. Remove your jars and let them cool before storing.

Nutrition per serving: Calories: 210| Carbs: 18g| Fat: 10g| Protein: 13g

11.5.7 Vegetable Soup

Serves: 4-pint jars | Prep Time: 10 minutes | Cook Time: 25 minutes

Ingredients:

- Corn – 1 pint jar
- Carrots – 1 pint jar
- Peas – 1 pint jar
- Peppers – 1 pint jar
- dried pasta - 1 c.
- Italian seasoning - 1 tsp
- Water

Procedure:

1. In a large pot, mix all canned vegetables with their canning liquid. Add water 1-inch above all vegetables and bring it to boil on medium-high flame and boil it for 15 minutes.

2. Mix in the pasta and Italian seasoning to add flavor. Allow to boil to make the pasta tender.

3. Transfer the soup to hot jars. Leave headspace of 1-inch. Clean the rim of the glass jar. Place the lid and apply a band around it. Adjust to ensure that the lid is tight.

4. Place jars on racks with simmering 2-inches water to 180 F in a pressure canner.

5. Place lid on canner, adjust medium-high heat. Vent steam for 10 minutes at 11 lbs. pressure for the dial gauge or 10 lbs. for the weighted-gauge canner.

6. Process the jars for 1 hour and 15 minutes. Turn off your canner, and remove the lid after two minutes when pressure turns zero. Keep the jars in the canner for 10 minutes more.

7. Remove your jars and let them cool before storing.

Nutrition per serving: Calories: 125 | Carbs: 20g | Fat: 3g | Protein: 10g

11.5.8 Canned Vegetable Soup

Serves: 6 quarts | Prep Time: 1 hr. | Cook Time: 1 hr. 20 mins

Ingredients:

- Peeled tomatoes - 4 c.
- Beef, chicken, or vegetable broth - 4½ quarts
- Peeled potatoes - 3 c.
- Whole kernel corn - 4 c.
- Sliced carrots - 2 c.
- Green beans - 2 c.
- Chopped onion - 1 c.
- Sliced celery - 2 c.
- Snipped parsley - 2 tbsp.
- Garlic - 3
- Snipped thyme - 1 tbsp.
- Snipped marjoram - 1 tbsp.
- Snipped rosemary - 1 tbsp.
- Pepper - ½ tsp.

Procedure:

1. Mix tomatoes, corn, broth, carrots, potatoes, green beans, onion, garlic, celery, parsley, thyme, marjoram, rosemary, and pepper in an 8- to 10-quart Dutch oven or kettle.
2. Bring to a boil, then turn off the heat. Cover and cook for 5 mins (vegetables will be crisp).
3. Fill hot, clean pint or quart canning jars approximately half-filled with heated veggies. Fill the container halfway with hot liquid, allowing a 1-inch headspace. Air bubbles should be removed, jar rims should be cleaned, and lids should be adjusted.
4. Process full jars in the pressure canner for 120 minutes for quarts or 60 min for pints at 10 lbs. of pressure for weighted canners and 11 lbs. pressure for the dial-gauge canners. Let the pressure naturally decrease.
5. Remove the jars from the canner and place them on racks to cool.

Nutrition per serving: Calories: 76 | Carbs 16g | Protein: 3g | Fat: 1g.

11.5.9 Chicken Mexican Soup Canning

Serves: 7 quarts | Prep Time: 1 hr. 30 mins | Cook Time: 1 hr. 15 mins

Ingredients:

- Boneless chicken breasts - 3 large
- Carrots - 1 1/2 c.
- Celery - 2 c.
- Onion chopped - 1 large
- Rotel Tomatoes - 2 (14 1/2 oz.) cans
- Kidney beans - 2 (15 oz.) cans
- Diced tomatoes - 4 c.
- Water - 6 c.
- Chicken broth - 6 c.
- Corn - 3 c.
- Ground cumin - 1 tsp.
- Canning salt - 1 tbsp.
- Garlic cloves - 3
- Chicken bouillon cubes - 3

Procedure:

1. Cook the chicken in a covered pot until it is done. You may shred the chicken or chop it into 1-inch cubes after it has cooled. Set aside.
2. Set up a pressure canner. In a saucepan of simmering water, heat the jars and lids until they are ready to use. (Do not bring to a boil.)
3. Except for the chicken, combine all the ingredients in big saucepan. Bring to boil, then reduce to low heat and cook for 3 minutes. Add the chicken and cook for 5 minutes on low heat.
4. Remove air bubbles and clean jar rims after ladling hot soup into the hot jars, leaving 1-inch headspace. Place the heated lid in the middle of the jar. Apply the band and tighten it with your fingers. In a pressure canner, place the jars.
5. Process quarts for 90 mins at 11 lbs. pressure or pints for 75 mins (adjust for the altitude if needed).
6. Remove the jars and set them aside to cool. After 24 hours, check the lids for seal. When the center of the lid is squeezed, it should not bend up and down.

Nutrition per serving: Calories: 371 | Carbs 46.4g | Protein: 28.5g | Fat: 9.4g.

11.5.10   Turkey Soup

Serves: 10 | Prep Time: 10 mins | Cook Time: 2 hrs.

Ingredients:

- Diced turkey - 3 1/2 c.
- Chicken stock - 16 c.
- Slice carrots - 1 1/2 c.
- Onion - 1 c.
- Diced celery - 1 1/2 c.
- Chicken bouillon – 2 tbsps.
- Salt – ¼ tsp.
- Pepper – ¼ tsp.

Procedure:

1. In a stockpot, combine all of the ingredients and bring to a boil. Prepare the jars as well as the lids. Fill heated jars halfway with soup, allowing 1" headspace. Make sure the jars are empty of air bubbles.
2. Put the lids and rings on after wiping the rims. Tighten your finger.
3. Prepare the pressure canner according to the manufacturer's instructions. Place jars in canner and process for 75 mins at 11 lbs. for pints and 90 mins for quarts in a dial gauge canner or 10 lbs. in a weighted gauge canner. Maintain constant pressure the entire time.
4. Before opening the canner, make sure the pressure has returned to zero.

Nutrition per serving: Calories: 260| Carbs 25g| Protein: 29g| Fat: 4.8g.

11.6 MEAT, PORK AND POULTRY

11.6.1 Buttered Chicken Breast

Serves: 8 pints | Prep time: 15 mins | Cook time: 2 hours

Ingredients

- boneless and skinless chicken breasts - 18 medium
- salt - 1 ½ tbsps.
- water - 4 ½ c.
- Butter or Olive Oil for frying in skillet – 1 tbsp.

Procedure

1. Cook each side of the chicken in a skillet with some butter or olive oil, about 8-10 minutes. Remove from the heat when the chicken is white and cooked all the way through. If you poke it with a fork, the juices should run clear.
2. In each pint jar, place a ½ tsp. of salt and 2 chicken breasts.
3. Fill the jar with water.
4. Can for 70 minutes at 10 lbs. of pressure for the weighted gauge of the pressure canner or 11 lbs. if the pressure canner has a dial gauge.
5. Remove the jars, and let cool until it is room temperature, which may take about a day.

Nutritional per serving: Calories: 45 Fat: 1g Carbs: 0g Protein: 9g

11.6.2 Pressure Canned Beef Short Rib

Serves: 12 half pint jars | Prep Time: 60 minutes | Cook Time: 75 minutes

Ingredients:

- Beef short rib - 10 lb.
- Water – 6 c.
- Pickling salt – 6 tsps.

Procedure:

1. Heat a skillet sprayed with cooking spray. Brown the short ribs and keep it covered in a bowl to keep it hot.

2. Pack the beef in sterilized jars leaving a headspace of 1-inch. Add a ½ tbsp. of pickling salt in each jar.
3. Add boiling water or stock to each jar, then remove the bubbles.
4. Set the rims and the lids. Transfer the jars to the pressure canner and process them at 10 lbs. for 75 minutes.
5. Wait for the pressure canner to depressurize to zero before removing the jars.
6. Set the jars on a cooling rack for 24 hours then store in a cool dry place.

Nutrition per serving: Calories: 205 fat 3.4g Carbs: 0g Protein: 28.9g Sugars: 0g

11.6.3 Pressure Canned Ground Beef

Serves: 12 pint jars | Prep Time: 50 minutes | Cook Time: 75 minutes

Ingredients:

- Ground beef - 12 lb.
- Water – 8 c.
- Pickling salt – 6 tsps.
- Cooking spray

Procedure:

1. Heat a skillet sprayed with cooking spray. Brown the ground beef and keep it in a covered bowl to keep them hot.
2. Pack the beef in sterilized jars leaving a headspace of 1-inch. Add a ½ tbsp. of pickling salt in each jar.
3. Add boiling water or stock, then remove the bubbles.
4. Wipe rims and set the lids on. Transfer the jars to the pressure canner and process them at 10 lbs. for 75 minutes.
5. Wait for the pressure canner to depressurize to zero before removing the jars.
6. Set the jars on a cooling rack for 24 hours then store in a cool dry place.

Nutrition per serving: Calories: 124 fats: 1.8g Carbs: 0g Protein: 21.2g Sugars: 0g Fiber: 0g Sodium: 62mg Potassium: 0mg

11.6.4 Beef in Wine Sauce

Serves: 3 pint jars | Prep Time: 40 minutes | Cook Time: 75 minutes

Ingredients:

- apple - 5 oz.
- carrot, shredded - 4 oz.
- onions - ¾ c.
- stewing beef - 2 lb.
- water - ¾ c.
- red wine - ½ c.
- salt - 1 tbsp.
- garlic cloves - 2
- beef bouillon cubes - 2
- bay leaves - 2
- kitchen bouquet - ½ tbsp.

Procedure:

1. Wash the apples thoroughly then core and shred them. Put them in a large pot.
2. Wash the carrots and peel them. Wash once more and shred them. Add them to the pot too.
3. Wash onions, peel and slice them into small pieces. Add the onions to the pot.
4. Cut the stewing beef into an inch size pieces and brown it on a skillet in batches over medium heat. Add the beef to the pot.
5. Add all other ingredients to the pot. Set everything to boil then reduce heat to low and simmer for 1 hour or until the meat is tender.
6. Remove the bay leaves and discard them. Ladle the mixture in sterilized jars leaving an inch headspace.
7. Remove the bubbles then wipe the rims with a clean damp towel.
8. Put on the lids and the rings on the jars. Transfer the jars to the pressure canner and process them at 10 lbs. pressure for 75 minutes.
9. Wait for the pressure canner to depressurize to zero before removing the jars.
10. Set the jars on a cooling rack for 24 hours then store in a cool dry place.

Nutrition per serving: Calories: 364 fat: 10.7g Carbs: 12.1g Protein: 49.1g Sugars: 7.7g Fiber: 2.1g Sodium: 709mg Potassium: 826mg

11.6.5 Beer Roast with Ketchup

Serves: 6 pint jars | Prep Time: 2 minutes | Cook Time: 1 hours 30 minutes

Ingredients:

- roast - 6 lbs.
- beer - 1 bottle
- onions, pureed - 2
- ketchup - 2 c.
- prepared yellow mustard - ¼ c.
- brown sugar - ½ c.
- apple cider vinegar - ¼ c.
- garlic powder - 1 tbsp.
- black pepper - 1 tsp.
- liquid smoke - 1 tbsp.
- Louisiana-style hot sauce - ½ tbsp.

Procedure:

1. Set the roast and onions in a slow cooker, then pour a bottle of beer over them.
2. Cook on low for 10 hours. The meat should be so delightfully tender that it falls apart when you touch it with a fork.
3. Smash the meat with two forks and set it to the cooking liquid in the slow cooker. Stir to combine.
4. In a saucepan, combine remaining ingredients with a whisk to make your sauce.
5. Stirring frequently, bring the sauce ingredients to a boil.
6. Spill the sauce over the meat in the slow cooker. Stir well. Heat the sauce on low for another 30 minutes.
7. Ladle the hot meat and sauce into sanitized jars.
8. Place lids on the jars and set in a pressure canner to process for 70 minutes at 10 PSI. If you are using quart jars, process at the same pressure for 90 minutes.

Nutrition per serving: Calories: 120 Sodium: 23 mg Fiber: 2.4g Fat: 2.1g Carbs: 1.3g Protein: 10.3g

11.6.6 Pork Carnitas with Bay Leaf

Serves: 15-pint jar | Prep Time: 13 minutes | Cook Time: 90 minutes

Ingredients:

- pork - 15 lbs.
- garlic, minced - 1 clove
- minced onion - ⅛ c.
- ground cumin - ½ tsp.
- chili powder - ½ tsp.
- dried oregano - ½ tsp.
- salt - ⅛ tsp.
- bay leaf - 1
- lime juice - 1 tbsp.

Procedure:

1. If necessary, cut pork into bite-sized pieces. Trim the visible fat off the roast.
2. Add pork to quart jars, allowing room for the additional ingredients.
3. Top each jar with the seasonings above in the order listed. Do not add any additional liquid.
4. Clean the jars with a paper towel dipped in vinegar, then put the lids on.
5. Process for 90 minutes using a pressure canner at 11 PSI.

Nutrition per serving: Calories: 104 Sodium: 33 mg Fiber: 1.4 g Fat: 4.1 g Carbs: 16.3 g Protein: 1.3 g

11.6.7 Lamb Pot

Serves: 2 pint jars | Prep Time: 13 minutes | Cook Time: 75 minutes

Ingredients:

- sliced onion - 1
- chopped rosemary sprigs - 2
- lamb or beef gravy - 2 c.
- canned lamb - 1 lb.
- black pepper – ¼ tsp.
- sliced potatoes - ¾ lb.
- water

Procedure:

1. Set potatoes in hot water and boil for 10 minutes.

2. Cook lamb in an ovenproof skillet for 5 minutes to brown. Heat broiler to medium.
3. Place onion and rosemary into skillet with lamb and cook for 3 minutes. Add in pepper and gravy and stir.
4. Drain potatoes and top with meat. Broil for 5 minutes.
5. Fill jars with lamb to 1 inch from the top.
6. Heat lids in hot water for 3 minutes; place lids on jars and tighten rings slightly.
7. Transfer the jars to canner and fill with water to the jar rings; add vinegar to the water.
8. Close and lock pressure canner and allow to boil over high heat, then add cooking weight to the top.
9. After 20 minutes, turn heat to medium and cook for 75 minutes.
10. Turn off heat and leave canner alone until it has cooled completely to room temperature.
11. After canner has cooled, remove jars from the canner and check for sealing.

Nutrition per serving: Calories: 327.1 Fat: 3.7g Carbs: 54.9g Protein: 20.4g

11.6.8 Canned Mustard Pork and Beans

Serves: 5-pint jars | Prep Time: 13 minutes | Cook Time: 75 minutes

Ingredients:

- navy beans - 2 lbs.
- chopped onions - 2
- salt pork - 8 pieces
- brown sugar - ¼ c.
- yellow mustard - 1 tbsp.
- honey - 2 tbsps.
- tomato sauce - 30 oz.
- water - 3 c.
- salt - 1 tbsp.

Procedure:

1. Preheat your pressure canner.
2. Place a half c. of navy beans in each jar. Divide the onions equally among the jars then add a piece of pork to each jar.
3. Heat a saucepan and add sugar, mustard, honey, salt, tomato sauce, and water. Bring the

mixture to boil. Ladle the sauce mixture to each jar.

4. Fill the jar with boiling water ensuring you Leave a headspace of 1-inch.

5. Rinse the jar rims and place the lids and rings on the jars.

6. Arrange the jars in the pressure canner and process at 10 lbs. for 75 minutes.

7. Wait for the pressure canner to depressurize before removing the jars.

Nutrition per serving: Calories: 130 Fat: 1g Carbs: 26g Protein: 5g

11.6.9 Beef Short Rib

Serves: 12-pint jars | Prep Time: 10 minutes | Cook Time: 10-12 minutes

Ingredients:

- beef short rib - 10 lbs.
- Water, as needed
- pickling salt as needed
- cooking spray

Procedure:

1. Heat a skillet sprayed with cooking spray. Brown the beef rib and keep it covered in a bowl to keep it hot.

2. Pack the beef in sterilized jars, leaving 1-inch headspace. Add a ½ tbsp of pickling salt to each jar. Add boiling water or stock to each jar, then remove the bubbles.

3. Rinse the rims and place the lids on. Transfer the jars to the pressure canner and process them at 10 lbs. for 1 hour and 15 minutes.

4. Wait for the pressure canner to depressurize to zero before removing the jars. Let it cool before storing.

Nutrition per serving: Calories: 205 | Carbs: 0 g | Fat: 9.1 g | Protein: 28.8 g

11.6.10 Beef Stroganoff

Serves: 4-pint jars | Prep Time: 20 minutes | Cook Time: 20 minutes

Ingredients:

- black pepper - 1 tsp
- salt - 2 tsps.

- thyme - 2 tsps.
- parsley - 2 tsps.
- Worcestershire sauce - 4 tbsps.
- garlic cloves, minced - 2
- mushrooms sliced - 1 c.
- onion chopped - 1 c.
- stewing beef - 2 lbs.
- beef broth - 4 c.

Procedure:

1. Sterilize the bottles in a pressure canner. Allow the bottles to cool before using.

2. In a saucepan, combine all fixings and bring to a boil for 5 mins. Adjust the heat to low, then continue cooking for another 20 minutes. Allow cooling slightly after turning off the heat.

3. Fill sterilized bottles with the mixture. Eliminate the air bubbles from the lid and close it.

4. Fill the pressure canner with the jars. Fill pressure canner halfway with water and process for 25 minutes. Let it cool before storing.

Nutrition Calories: 207 | Carbs: 5.1g | Fat: 6.1g | Protein: 33.5g

11.6.11 Meatballs

Serves: 6-pint jars | Prep Time: 5 minutes | Cook Time: 5 minutes

Ingredients:

- 2 lbs. ground meat
- 2 tsps. salt
- herbs of your choice, as needed
- tomato juice, as needed
- water

Procedure:

1. In a mixing dish, combine the herbs, meat, and salt. Mix until everything is properly blended.

2. In your saucepan, bring enough water to a boil. Form balls from the crushed beef mixture and carefully put them into boiling water.

3. Let it cook for 5 minutes before straining the meatballs.

4. Pack the meatballs into the sterilized bottles gently. Over the meatballs, pour enough

tomato liquid to cover them. Allow an inch of headspace. Close the lid after removing the air bubbles.

5. In the pressure canner, place the jars. Fill the pressure canner halfway with water and process for 30 minutes.
6. Turn off your canner, and remove the lid after two minutes when pressure turns zero.
7. Keep the jars in the canner for 10 minutes more. Remove your jars and let them cool before storing.

Nutrition per serving: Calories: 272| Carbs: 0.8g| Fat: 14g| Protein: 35.8g

11.6.12 Canned Chicken Breast

Serves: 5-pint jars | Prep Time: 5 minutes | Cook Time: 0 minutes

Ingredients:

- chicken breast, sliced into small pieces - 5 lbs.
- Salt, as needed

Procedure:

1. Place the chicken in the sterilized jars leaving 1-inch headspace. Add a ½ tbsp. of salt to each jar.
2. Get rid of the air bubbles and wipe the jar rims with a damp cloth. Put the lids and the rings on the jars. Transfer the jars to the pressure canner and process them at 10 lbs. pressure for 1 hour and 15 minutes.
3. Wait for the pressure canner to depressurize to zero before removing the jars. Let it cool before storing.

Nutrition per serving: Calories: 120| Carbs: 2.5 g| Fat: 2.5 g| Protein: 25 g

11.6.13 Pot Roast

Serves: 2 quart jars | Prep Time: 15 mins | Cook Time: 50 mins

Ingredients:

- Ground black pepper - 1 tsp.
- Salt - 2 tsps.
- Stewing beef and cut into chunks - 2 lbs.
- Chopped onions - 1 c.

- Dried thyme - 2 tsps.
- Garlic minced - 2 cloves
- Bay leaves - 2
- Beef broth – 1 c.
- Dry red wine – 1 c.
- Chopped carrots - 1 c.
- Diced potatoes - 1 c.
- Chopped celery - ½ c.

Procedure:

1. As directed in the basic rules of this eBook, sterilize the bottles in a pressure canner. Let the bottles to cool before using.
2. In a large saucepan, combine the meat, thyme, onions, bay leaves, garlic, broth, black pepper, wine & salt to taste. Turn the heat on and close the lid. Bring to a boil for 10 minutes, then reduce to low heat for another 10 minutes.
3. Add the veggies and cook for a further 5 minutes. Turn the heat off.
4. Fill sterilized bottles with the mixture.
5. Pop the air bubbles in the lid and seal it.
6. Fill the pressure canner with the jars. Fill pressure canner halfway with water and process for 25 mins.

Nutrition per serving: Calories: 234| Carbs 9.3g| Protein: 34.2g| Fat: 6.2g.

11.6.14 Chipotle Beef

Serves: 2 (quart) jars | Prep Time: 15 mins | Cook Time: 48 mins

Ingredients:

- Beef brisket and cut into chunks - 2 lbs.
- Salt - 2 tsps.
- Garlic - 8 cloves
- Onion chopped - 2 c.
- Black pepper – 1 tsp.
- Oregano - 2 tsp.
- Coriander - ½ c.
- Chipotle chilies - 2
- Beef broth - 4 c.

Procedure:

1. As directed in the basic rules of this eBook, sterilize the bottles in a pressure canner. Allow all bottles to cool before using.
2. Season the meat with salt and pepper in a saucepan. Turn on the heat & sear for 3 minutes on both sides. Combine the onion and garlic in a mixing bowl. Cook for a further minute. Combine the remaining ingredients in a mixing bowl.
3. Simmer the beef for 20 minutes over medium heat with the lid closed. Remove the pan from the heat and set it aside to cool slightly.
4. Fill the bottles with the mixture.
5. Pop the air bubbles in the lid and seal it.
6. Fill the pressure canner with the jars. Fill pressure canner halfway with water and process for 25 mins.

Nutrition per serving: Calories: 322| Carbs 5.4g| Protein: 22.9g| Fat: 22.6g.

11.6.15   Canned Goulash

Serves: 2 (quart) jars | Prep Time: 15 mins | Cook Time: 45 mins

Ingredients:

- Stewing beef and cut into chunks - 4 lbs.
- Peppercorns - 20
- Bay leaves - 3
- Caraway seeds - 2 tsps.
- Vegetable oil - 1/3 c.
- Onions chopped - 3
- Salt - 1 tbsp.
- Celery stalks - 6
- Carrots, peeled & chopped - 4
- Mustard powder - 2 tsps.
- Water - 1 ½ c.
- Vinegar - 1/3 c.

Procedure:

1. Use a pressure canner to sterilize the bottles. Allow bottles to cool before using.
2. Combine the meat, bay leaves, peppercorns, and caraway seeds in a mixing dish. Allow the meat to marinate for an hour in the refrigerator.
3. In a medium saucepan, heat the oil. Stir in the seasoned meat after one minute of sautéing the

onions until aromatic. Before adding the remainder of the ingredients, season with salt to taste.
4. Bring to boil for 5 mins with the lid closed. Cook for 15 minutes on low heat. Allow cooling slightly after turning off the heat.
5. Fill the bottles with the mixture.
6. Remove air bubbles from the lid and shut it. Fill the pressure canner with the jars. Fill pressure canner halfway with water and process for 25 mins.

Nutrition per serving: Calories: 69| Carbs 13g| Protein: 29g| Fat: 12g.

11.6.16   Chicken Taco Meat for Pressure Canning

Serves: 7 quarts | Prep Time: 30 mins | Cook Time: 90 mins

Ingredients:

- Chicken - 14 lbs.
- Large onion - 1
- Poblano peppers - 4
- Onion powder - 2 tbsps.
- Mexican oregano - 2 tbsps.
- Kosher salt - 1 1/2 tbsp.
- Garlic powder - 3 tbsp.
- Ground cumin - 1 tbsp.
- Chili powder - 3 tbsps.
- Cayenne pepper - 2 tsp.
- Chicken broth or Filtered water
- Water

Procedure:

1. In hot, soapy water, wash the jars, lids, and rings. Fill the pressure canner with water according to the instructions of your computer.
2. Combine the onions, chicken, peppers, and all of the spices and herbs in a large mixing bowl. Uniformly coating
3. Remove any air bubbles and leave 1 inch headspace in the jars. If necessary, add a little cold water or cold chicken broth to get a 1 inch headspace. Wipe rims and fingertip-tighten lids and rings. Cold jars should be placed in a cold canner.

4. Process for 90 mins for quarts and 75 mins for pints.

Nutrition per serving: Calories: 12| Carbs 3g| Protein: 9g| Fat: 8g.

11.6.17 Beef Chunks

Serves: 4-pint jars | Prep Time: 30 minutes | Cook Time: 1 hour 30 minutes

Ingredients:

- beef chunks - 3 lbs.
- beef broth - 4 pints

Procedure:

1. Begin by browning your meat pieces in a big, clean pan over medium heat.
2. Bring the broth to a boil in a medium-sized saucepan while the meat cooks.
3. Make sure the meat is completely cooled before putting it in your jars, then seal them up tightly. Pour the heated liquid over the meat while maintaining a reasonable headspace.
4. Set jars in the pressure canner and set the timer for 75 minutes, depending on your elevation.
5. After cooking, let the jars cool fully before handling.

Nutrition per serving: Calories 162| Fat 2.4g, Sodium 57mg, Potassium 271mg, Carbs 0g

11.7 SEAFOOD

11.7.1 Smoked & Cured Salmon

Serves: 5 | Prep Time: 3 days & 20 minutes | Cook time: 2 minutes

Ingredients:

- kosher salt - 2 1/2 tbsp.
- light brown sugar - 2 tbsps.
- salmon fillet, center-cut - 1 (2 lbs.)
- ground coriander - 1 tsp.
- vodka - 2 tbsps.
- zest from 1 orange

Procedure:

1. Smoke the salmon on high heat with desired flavored wood chips for 20 seconds, flip and smoke for 20 seconds more.
2. In a glass dish, place salmon skin side up. Mix the rest of the ingredients and rub all over the salmon.
3. Cover and keep in the fridge for 3 days, flipping each day.
4. Rinse & cut into fillets. Serve.

Nutrition per serving: Calories 321 Protein 33 g Carbs 6 g

11.7.2 Smoked Sablefish or Black Cod

Serves: 10 | Prep Time: 2 days & 20 minutes | Cook time: 4 hours

Ingredients:

- kosher salt - 1 c.
- Honey
- sugar - 1/4 c.
- Sweet paprika
- sablefish fillets, with skin - 3 lbs.
- garlic powder - 2 tbsps.

Procedure:

1. In a bowl, mix the garlic powder, salt & sugar.
2. Add a layer of spice mix at the bottom of the container.
3. Add the fish fillet skin side down.

4. Add the rest of the spice mix on top, rub it into the skin.
5. Cover and keep in the fridge about as many hours as the weight of the fillets.
6. Rinse the fish & pat dry. Keep in the fridge, overnight & uncovered.
7. Smoke the fish for 2-3 hours at 160 F.
8. Brush the fish with honey after every 60 minutes. Cool & debone the fish.
9. Add paprika on top. Serve chilled

Nutrition per serving: Calories 156 Protein 35 g Carbs 12 g

11.7.3 Pickled Mackerel

Serves: 10 | Prep Time: 3 days & 20 minutes | Cook time: 0 minutes

Ingredients:

- frozen mackerels, (thawed) halves without tail & head - 4
- lemon - 6 slices
- cooking salt - 3/4 c.
- rice vinegar - 2 c.

Procedure:

1. Rinse & pat dry. Cover the fish with salt in a thin layer. Let it rest for 1.5 hours.
2. Rinse & pat dry; add to a zip lock bag with lemon slices & vinegar.
3. Keep in the fridge for 2 hours to 3 days.
4. Take the fish out and peel the skin; take the bones out as well.
5. Serve.

Nutrition per serving: Calories 165 Protein 13 g Carbs 3 g

11.7.4 Seafood Raminara

Serves: 1 | Prep Time: 20 minutes | Cook time: 10 minutes

Ingredients:

- ramen noodles - ½ pack
- water - 1 c.

- dried shrimp - ¼ c.
- tomato sauce leather - ¼ c.
- dried vegetables - ¼ c.
- parmesan cheese - 2 tbsps.

Procedure:

1. In a bowl, add water with the rest of the ingredients except for cheese. Let it rest for 5 minutes.
2. Boil and cook for 1 minute. Turn off the heat, allow to rest for 10 minutes.
3. Add parmesan before serving.

Nutrition per serving: Calories 231 Protein 12 g Carbs 11 g

11.7.5 Smoked Sturgeon

Serves: 8 | Prep Time: 20 minutes | Cook time: 15 minutes

Ingredients:

- sturgeon, cut into large pieces - 5 lbs.
- mace - 1 tsp.
- kosher salt - 1 c.
- Brandy, as needed
- sugar - 1/4 c.
- garlic powder - 1 tbsp.

Procedure:

1. Trim & cut the fish.
2. Using a bowl, add in mace, garlic powder, kosher salt and sugar and mix, then coat the fish.
3. Let it rest in a container as much as it weighs.
4. Rinse & pat dry. Brush with brandy. Keep in the fridge uncovered for 1 day.
5. Smoke for 4 hours at 160 F.
6. Store in a vacuum seal bag for up to 6 months.

Nutrition per serving: Calories 51 Protein 7 g Carbs 1 g

11.7.6 Simple Seafood Curry

Serves: 1 | Prep Time: 20 minutes | Cook time: 10 minutes

Ingredients:

- cooked basmati rice (dehydrated) - 1/4 c.

- dehydrated seafood mix - 1/4 c.
- coconut milk powder - 3 tbsp.
- Thai yellow curry paste, dehydrated - 1 tsp.
- tomato sauce powder - 2 tbsp.

Procedure:

1. In a pot, add all ingredients with 1¼ c. of water.
2. Boil on medium flame.
3. Cook for 5 minutes, stirring often. Turn the heat off, let it rest for 10 minutes.

Nutrition per serving: Calories 631 Protein 25.1 g Carbs 55.4 g

11.7.7 Quinoa & Crab Curry

Serves: 1 | Prep Time: 20 minutes | Cook time: 15 minutes

Ingredients:

- Thai yellow curry paste, dehydrated - 1 tsp.
- cooked & dehydrated quinoa - 1/4 c.
- coconut milk powder - 2 tbsp.
- dehydrated imitation crab - 1/4 c.

Procedure:

1. In a pot, add all ingredients with 1 ¼ c. of water.
2. Boil on medium flame.
3. Cook for 5 minutes, stirring often. Turn off the heat, allow to rest for 10 minutes.

Nutrition per serving: Calories 539 Protein 14.8 g Carbs 46 g

11.7.8 McDonald's Pressure Canned Fish

Serves: 10 pints | **Prep time:** 20 minutes | **Cook time:** 0 minutes

Ingredients

- 11" blue backs - 20
- Onions - 3
- pickling salt - 2 tbsps.
- white vinegar - 9 tbsps.
- ketchup - 9 tbsps.

Procedure:

1. Clean the fish, remove the skin, and cut it into 2 chunks.

2. In a small bowl, mix salt, vinegar and ketchup.

3. Now layer the ingredients in the sterilized jars such that you start with fish, onions, and a tablespoon of the vinegar mixture. Repeat with all the jars leaving a headspace of 1/4 inch.

4. Wipe the rims and place the lids and the rings on the jars.

5. Place the jars in the pressure canner and process them at 11 lb for 100 minutes.

6. Wait for the pressure canner to depressurize to zero before removing the jars.

7. Place the jars on a cooling rack for 24 hours then store in a cool dry place.

Nutrition per serving: Calories 139, fat 4.1g, Protein 25, carbs 0g Sugars 0g, Fiber 0g, Sodium 560mg, Potassium 0mg

11.7.9 Pressure Canned Tuna

Serves 6 pints | **Prep time:** 20 minutes | **Cook time:** 0 minutes

Ingredients

- tuna - 5 lbs.
- salt
- vegetable oil

Procedure:

1. Use a sharp kitchen knife to peel off the skin then scrape the surface to remove the blood vessels.
2. Cut the fish lengthwise, then into pieces that fit in a pint jar.
3. Add salt in each jar.
4. If you have precooked the tuna, add the fish, some vegetable oil, and a tablespoon of salt per pint jar.

5. Wipe the rims and place the lids and the rings on the jars. Process the jars at 10 pounds pressure for 100 minutes.
6. Wait for the pressure canner to depressurize to zero before removing the jars.
7. Place the jars on a cooling rack for 24 hours then store in a cool dry place.

Nutrition per serving: Calories 191, fat 1.4g, carbs 0g Protein 42, Sugars 0g, Fiber 0g, Sodium 83mg, Potassium 0mg

11.7.10   Pressure canned Whole clams

Serves 7 pints | **Prep time:** 20 minutes | **Cook time:** 10 minutes

Ingredients

- Clam - 5 lbs.
- salt - 3 tbsps.
- lemon juice - 2 tbsps.
- Water

Procedure:

1. Keep the clams cold in ice until you are ready to pressure can them.
2. Scrub the shells then stream them over water for 5 minutes. Open the clams and remove meat. Save the juices.
3. Add a gallon of water in a mixing bowl then add at most 3 tablespoons of salt. Wash the clam meat in the salted water.
4. Add water in a shallow saucepan then add lemon juice. Bring the water to boil. Add the clam meat and boil for 2 minutes.
5. Heat the reserved clam juices until boiling.
6. Drain the meat and pack it loosely in the jars leaving 1-inch headspace. Pour the hot clam juice over the meat then remove the bubbles.
7. You may add boiling water if you run out of the clam juice.
8. Wipe the rims and place the lids and the rings on the jars. Process the jars at 10 pounds pressure for 60 minutes
9. Wait for the pressure canner to depressurize to zero before removing the jars.
10. Place the jars on a cooling rack for 12-24 hours undisturbed then store in a cool dry place.

Nutrition per serving: Calories 148, fat 2g, carbs 5.1g Protein 25.5, Sugars 0g, Fiber 0g,

11.7.11   Pressure Canned Minced Clams

Serves: 5 pints | **Prep time:** 20 minutes | **Cook time:** 0 minutes

Ingredients

- Clam - 5 lbs.
- salt - 3 tbsps.
- lemon juice - 2 tbsps.
- Water

Procedure:

1. Keep the clams cold in ice until you are ready to pressure can them.
2. Scrub the shells then stream them over water for 5 minutes. Open the clams and remove meat. Save the juices.
3. Add a gallon of water in a mixing bowl then add at most 3 tablespoons of salt. Wash the clam meat in the salted water.
4. Add water in a shallow saucepan then add lemon juice. Bring the water to boil. Add the clam meat and boil for 2 minutes.
5. Heat the reserved clam juices until boiling.
6. Drain the meat and add it to the grinder or a food processor.
7. Pack 3/4 cup of minced clams in a half-pint leaving a headspace of 1- inch. Add the clam juices maintaining the headspace.
8. Remove any air bubbles and add more clam juice if necessary. In case you run out of clam juice, add boiling water.
9. Wipe the rims and place the lids and the rings on the half-pint jars. Process the jars at 10 pounds pressure for 60 minutes
10. Wait for the pressure canner to depressurize to zero before removing the jars.
11. Place the jars on a cooling rack undisturbed then store in a cool dry place

Nutrition per serving: Calories 148, fat 2g, carbs 5.1g Protein 25.5, Sugars 0g, Fiber 0g,

11.7.12   Pressure Canned Shrimp

Serves 10 pints | **Prep time:** 20 minutes | **Cook time:** 0 minutes

Ingredients

- Shrimp - 10 lbs.
- salt - 1/4 c.
- vinegar - 1 c.
- water

Procedure:

1. Remove the heads immediately you catch shrimp then chill until ready to preserve them.
2. Wash the shrimps and drain them well.
3. Add a gallon of water in a pot then add salt and vinegar. Bring to boil then cook shrimp for 10 minutes.
4. Use a slotted spoon to remove the shrimp from cooking liquid then rinse it in cold water and drain . Peel the shrimp while packing it in the sterilized jars.
5. Add a gallon of water with 3 tablespoon salt and bring it to a boil. Add the brine to the jars and remove the air bubbles. Add more brine if necessary.
6. Wipe the jar rims with a cloth damped in vinegar. Place the lids and the rings.
7. Process the jars at 10 pounds pressure for 45 minutes
8. Wait for the pressure canner to depressurize to zero before removing the jars.
9. Place the jars on a cooling rack undisturbed then store in a cool dry place

Nutrition per serving: Calories 100, fat 2g, carbs 1g Protein 15g, Sugars 0g, Fiber 0g

12 CONCLUSION

Having read this book, you should have a good idea of the different types of canning jars and how to use them for home canning. You now have an idea about the amazing canning world. Do not be disheartened by all this information, I do not want to scare you. It is essential that you follow all our rules and you will be amazed by the results that you will get. Nowadays knowing the basis of canning and preserving is very important. Remember, like other kitchen utensils, the right canning jar size must be selected so that you only use it for the food you are preserving.

When you're ready to cook, choose the right canning jar. When you do, it will be easier to preserve your foods safely in jars. Also, you can find many different jars that are ideal for preserving a range of foods such as jams, jellies, applesauce and even baby food.

This book is written to help you to become a real pro in canning and preserving. As the time goes by you will not need this book anymore because your mistake will decrease. Do not be impatient, you will have to start in small steps and you will gradually succeed in preserving your products. Indeed, you will be able to create your own recipes without the assistance of our book.

Canning is a skill that you need know in order to prepare healthy food for your family and your friends. Finally, if you're new to home canning and want to get started with water bath canning, consider practicing with all the recipes in this book. If you do not try and fail, you will never learn. Thank you and be careful!

Sarah Roslin

Lightning Source UK Ltd.
Milton Keynes UK
UKHW050029071022
410070UK00015B/99